FRANTIŠEK MEZIHORÁK

GALLERY
OF GREAT
EUROPEANS

FRANTIŠEK MEZIHORÁK

GALLERY
OF GREAT
EUROPEANS

NAKLADATELSTVÍ
OLOMOUC

2003

Acknowledgements

I would like to thank PhDr D. Skoupá, CSc. Mgr L. Novotná
and Mgr J. Sejvalová for the subsidiary role they played in the preparation
of this book.

Jacket design by Ivana Perůtková.

Portraits of P. Du Bois, E. Crucé and Ch. Saint-Pierre created by Inka Delevová.

Language correction by Simon and Nora Gill.

Published by: NAKLADATELSTVÍ OLOMOUC
Lazecká 70a, Olomouc 772 00
Tel.: +420 585 224 037, 585 204 377
Fax.: +420 585 231 720
E-mail: olomouc@mbox.vol.cz
Internet address: http://www.nakladatelstvi-ol.cz

1st edition NAKLADATELSTVÍ OLOMOUC, 2003

ISBN 80-7182-149-7

CONTENTS

CONTENTS

Contents

ADENAUER KONRAD

* 1876 Cologne   † 1963 Rhöndorf

"I regard it as a very promising sign, and maybe even a sign of Providence, that the whole immensity of actions, which must be weighed, rests upon the shoulders of men, who are filled with the desire to build a new Europe on a Christian basis. I believe that only a few events in the history of Europe offered a better opportunity to achieve such an aim. ... In my opinion, the European nation state has a history, but it has no future. This holds true in the political and the economic spheres, as well as in the social sphere. Not one single European country may secure the safety of its people solely by its own means. I consider the Schuman Plan and the European Defence Community to be preparatory steps for the political unification of Europe."

• German lawyer, politician and statesman • from a Catholic clerk's family in the Rhineland • studies of law and economics in Freiburg, Munich, and Bonn • 1902-1906 associate justice and advocate in Cologne • from 1906 town councillor for the Catholic party Zentrum in Cologne • 1917-1933 chief mayor of Cologne • from 1920 member of the Prussian Council of State, later its president • adversary of National Socialism • 1933 removed from all functions by the Nazis • 1944 imprisoned after the attempted assassination of Hitler • after the war co-founder of the Christian Democratic Union (CDU) • March 1946 after the election victory of the CDU at the head of West German politics • 1948 president of the Parliamentary Council - participation in

ADENAUER KONRAD

compiling the new German constitution • 1949-1966 chairman of the CDU • 15 September 1949 elected the first Chancellor of the Federal Republic of Germany (FRG) - remained in office until 1963 •

Konrad Adenauer became well known as a sharp and realistic politician, who was stubbornly focused on enforcing his aims, as well as a man who always bravely defended his ideas and beliefs. His main target, based on the tragic experience of the Nazi era, was to integrate the FRG into the western European political and economic system. He considered especially important the establishment of a new relationship with France. He played an important role in the integration of the FRG into many international organizations. His significant successes included, for instance, the Paris Agreements of 1954, which brought the acknowledgement of the full sovereignty of the FRG and its integration into NATO, the termination of the war footing with the USSR, the establishment of diplomatic relations with the USSR, agreement about the return of German POWs, and the incorporation of the Saarland into the FRG. The western politician closest to Adenauer was Charles de Gaulle. Adenauer's era laid the foundations for a denazified and democratic Federal Republic of Germany and for its equal integration into western European structures. Under Adenauer's government, the traditional German-French hostility ceased, relations with Israel were rectified, and the country set forth on a way to European integration. He was one of those politicians who played the most important role in the development of the European communities, in which he saw a perspective for both the new Germany and the whole continent, which, through Europeanism, would be deprived of its fears of Germany once and for all.

For Europe - Peace and Freedom. Cologne 1954.
World Indivisible, with Liberty and Justice for all. London 1956.
Memoirs 1945-1953. Stuttgart 1966.
Memoirs. London 1966.
Erinnerungen. Frankfurt a. M. 1967.
Erinnerungen 1953-1955. Frankfurt a. M. 1968.
Erinnerungen 1959-1963. Stuttgart 1968.
Teegespräche 1955-1958. Berlin 1986.
Seid wach für die kommenden Jahre. Bergisch Gladbach 1997.
Die Demokratie ist für uns eine Weltanschauung. Köln 1998.

9

BAADER FRANZ XAVER VON

* 1765 Munich   † 1841 Munich

"The only salvation of European society is a Christian rapprochement of nations based on new warm relations between religion and politics."

• Bavarian Catholic philosopher, outstanding representative of philosophical Romanticism • studies of medicine in Ingolstadt and Vienna • from 1784 assistant to his father - a forensic surgeon • 1792-1796 studies of mineralogy in London, at the same time private studies of books on philosophy and theology • 1826 Professor of philosophy and speculative theology at Munich University - a tendency to overcome the contradiction between faith and science by fideism • 1827-1841 lectures in archeology at Munich University •

Together with other Catholic Romanticists (Novalis, J. Görres, F. Schlegel, F. W. Schelling et al.), he dreamed of a religious revival in Europe. But he did not understand it as being based on the defeat of Protestantism and he did not lay down conditions for its coming back to the pale of the Roman church; he believed in the reconciliation of Christian religions. In 1814 he sent an appeal to the Austrian Emperor, the Russian Tsar, and the Prussian King to establish a Christian European association and a union of the three main faiths which were represented by the monarchs (Catholicism, Protestantism, and Orthodoxy). In the process of European integration he attributed a major role to Russia, which he did not see as a submissive heretic or barbarian; therefore he was perceived as a German defender of Slavophile Russian messianism.

Gesellschaftslehre. München 1957.
Vom Sinn der Gesellschaft. Schriften zur Sozial-Philosophie. Köln 1966.
Gedanken über Staat und Gesellschaft, Revolution und Reform. Darmstadt 1968.
Schriften Franz von Baaders. Frankfurt a. M. 1980.
Sämtliche Werke. Aalen 1987.

BELLOC GEORGE HILAIRE PETER

* 1870 La Celle-Saint-Claud   † 1953 Guildford

"In other words, my thesis is as follows: the culture and civilisation of Christianity - i. e. what we have called Europe for centuries - were called into existence by the Catholic Church, which took over the social tradition of the Greek-Roman Empire and affected it, granted this huge organism new life. It was the Catholic Church which gave us shape. It gave us our unity and overall philosophy of life and it created the character of the white race."

• English Catholic writer - very talented and knowledgeable, endowed with rich imagination
• author of poems, novels, and literature for children and brilliant satires
• till 1887 upbringing in France • 1887-1892 stay at the family's manor in England, journey to the USA, military service in the French army
• from 1892 studies of history at Oxford • after 1897 study stays and lecturing in the USA, France, Italy • prolific publishing activity • monographs on historic personalities (Danton, Napoleon, Richelieu) • political essays ("Europe and Faith") • from 1937 visiting Professor of history in New York •

In his essays, written in the name of the church and European noblemen of the Middle Ages, he condemned the cult of science and progress. He placed Catholic culture high above other cultures (e. g. Islamic - "barbaric") and he considered the period of the 11th-13th centuries its grand era. He saw the Reformation as a disaster, the beginning of decay, and a greater and greater threat to Europe. He could not find

any positive results of man gaining deeper understanding of and control over the natural world. On the contrary, alongside social and national conflicts, he blamed it for the chaos or even the collapse of human
society at the beginning of the 20th century. For Europe in its crisis, he
thought, there was only one alternative, the re-establishment of the
Catholic faith, which would unite and restore the Continent.

The French Revolution. London 1915.
A General Sketch of the European War. London 1916.
Cesta do Říma [A Journey to Rome]. Praha 1920.
The Crisis of our Civilisation. New York 1958.
Europe and the Faith. Rockford 1992.

BENDA JULIEN

* 1867 Paris   † 1956 Fontenay-aux-Roses

"Europe has never yet known an awareness of political unity. From the political point of view every token of its will was orientated in an exclusively nationalistic way. ... In the spiritual and political spheres, the 20th century, which may witness the forming of Europe, began with a radical triumph of anti-Europe. ... Nowadays, the idea of nations seems to have reached the end of its road and to be harmful for Europeans; on the stage there appears the idea of Europe. But let us not cherish any illusions, let us not think this idea is going to win in quite a natural way; be sure that from the side of those who are going to lose their thrones as a result of it the idea will encounter tough resistance, tough obstacles."

• French philosopher, essayist, writer • uncompleted studies of engineering at the Sorbonne • existence as a rentier • defender of the intellectual traditions of reason and truth • passionately engaged in achieving justice in the Dreyfus scandal - criticism of the judiciary • critic and opponent of Bergson's intuitionism • supporter of rationalism • fighter for democracy and against totalitarianism • after WWII supports communism, but later a critic of political trials in the Soviet bloc •

By his polemics and appeals, by hard and critical words, he wanted to wake up Europe so that it could realize how serious the situation in which it found itself, in his opinion, really was. He doubted whether it was aware of itself and its mission to create unity. In all of history, from

Charlemagne till his own day, he could see the triumph of nationalism and divisive tendencies which, especially in the 19th century, took the form of "nations obsessed by divorce". He could see exemplary anti-European tendencies in Bismarck, who took every idea of a united Europe as stupid idealism. He criticized "the encapsulation of states" in the cult of themselves, their "sacred egoism" and "contempt for reason", which should result in unity. He supposed that that was why no real history of Europe had been written so far (with only one exception: the works of the Belgian Henri Pirenn), only a history of its parts, its differences, and its contradictions. He failed to find any awareness of the spiritual unity of our continent and only in the 18th century did he find an awareness of the spirit of Europe, with men such as Voltaire or Goethe. In his own day he could find the "infection of intellectual nationalism" even among his best contemporaries.

Zrada vzdělanců [A Betrayal of Educated People]. Praha 1929.
Velká zkouška demokracií. Povaha, historie a filosofická hodnota demokratických zásad [A Great Test of Democracies. The Nature, History, and Philosophical Value of Democratic Principles]. Praha 1947.
La crise du rationalisme. Paris 1949.
L'esprit européen. Neuchâtel 1957.
Discours à la nation européenne. Paris 1992.

BENEŠ EDVARD

* 1884 Kožlany   † 1948 Sezimovo Ústí

"By firm and principled policy it was possible to make from the Geneva institution a great instrument against any aggression. ... But it did not mean, as a lot of my opponents concluded at that time, that I trusted blindly in the effectiveness of the League of Nations under any circumstances and that I pinned all my hopes on it. ... I would like to add that this kind of concept of European international policy, along with agreement on systematic cooperation with the Soviet Union against aggressiveness and reaction in Germany, necessarily called for Western Europe's comprehension of the necessity for some adjustment of the social policy of Western Europe to conditions in the Soviet Union ... and at the same time for the Soviet Union seriously thinking of some adjustment of Soviet political and revolutionary conditions to conceptions of political freedom in Western Europe. ... It seemed to me that European and world peace called for it without fail and that it was worth these concessions."

• Czechoslovak politician and statesman • studies at the Faculty of Arts of Charles University in Prague • 1908 Doctorate in Law in Dijon • 1909 Doctorate in Philosophy in Prague • teacher at the Academy of Business • from 1913 senior lecturer (later Professor) of sociology at Prague University • 1914-1915 organizer of a resistance organization called "Maffia" • 1915 exile in Switzerland • from 1916 at the head of the Czechoslovak National Council in Paris • 1918-1919 Czechoslovak representative at the Paris Peace Conference • co-founder of the League of Nations • organizer of the Little Entente • 1918-1935 Minister of Foreign Affairs (in 1921-1922 Prime Minister as well) • 1935-1938 President of the CSR • resignation and exile after the Munich agreement between the four superpowers in 1938 • 1939 Professor at Chicago University • 1939-1945 London - political activity aimed at re-establishing the CSR • 1940 creator of the Czechoslovak exile government in exile; office of the President again • 1945-1948 President of the CSR • resigned in June 1948 •

Being Masaryk's true disciple, he believed in the European way of thinking and, in accordance with Masaryk's precepts, he could see that the peace system in Europe was extremely important, especially for a small state like the Czechoslovak Republic. His diplomatic activities in the office of the Minister of Foreign Affairs and later of the President of the state consistently supported all the tendencies that spoke for the unity of Europe. From the inception of the League of Nations he took part in its activities to an extent that brought him noticeable respect; he was also elected a member of its Board. He became the guiding spirit of the committee of the League of Nations which prepared the system of collective security and mutual assistance in Europe. Besides the British Prime Minister MacDonald and the French Premier E. Herriot, it was he who, to a large extent, contributed to the fact that in 1924 the League of Nations accepted unanimously the Geneva Memorandum, which declared war an international crime and requested the peaceful solution of disagreements and the reduction of armaments, and, consequently, even complete disarmament. Unfortunately, this document remained nothing but a beautiful dream. He was also disappointed by further seemingly hopeful diplomatic acts and his ideas of the Soviet Union's participation in the European democratic peace system remained mere illusions, too. When he repeatedly declared his conviction that the ideas of the League of Nations were bound to succeed and therefore it was not necessary to despair of partial failures, he could not fathom how much he himself would be exposed to a confrontation of European ideals with Hitler and Stalin's attempts to make Europe totalitarian.

Civilizace, její následky, léčení jich a jiné studie [Civilization, Its Consequences, Their Treatment and Other Studies]. Praha 1910.

K budoucímu míru [On Future Peace]. Praha 1919.

Locarno a svaz národů [Locarno and the League of Nations]. Praha 1925.

Problém malých národů po světové válce [The Problem of Small Nations after the World War]. Praha 1926.

O problému omezení zbrojení z hlediska politického, sociálního a hospodářského [On the Issue of Limiting Armaments from the Political, Social and Economic Points of View]. Praha 1929.

Anšlus nebo nová Europa? ["Anschluss" or New Europe?] Praha 1931.

Je možný trvalý mír? [Is Lasting Peace Possible?] Praha 1931.

Building a New Europe. London 1939.

Democracy Today and Tomorrow. London 1939.

International Security. Chicago 1939.

The New Central Europe. Chicago 1941.

The Organization of Postwar Europe. New York 1941.

Šest let exilu a druhé světové války [Six Years of Exile and World War II]. Praha 1946.

Úvahy o slovanské politice [Considerations of Slavonic Politics]. Praha 1947.

Demokracie dnes a zítra [Democracy Today and Tomorrow]. Praha 1948.

Paměti. Od Mnichova k nové válce a k novému vítězství [Memoires. From "Munich" to a New War and a New Victory]. Praha 1948.

Mnichovské dny. Paměti [The Days of "Munich". Memoirs]. Praha 1968.

Otevřít Rusko Evropě. Dvě stati k ruské otázce v r. 1922 [To Open Russia for Europe. Two Articles on the Russian Issue in the Year 1922]. Jinočany 1992.

BENTHAM JEREMY

* 1748 London   † 1832 London

"Do not let us have objections to the fact that the present days are not yet ready for such a suggestion (the unification of nations and everlasting peace - F. M.); the more they lack their maturity, the sooner we have to start doing anything that can be done to bring them to maturity. ... This kind of suggestion is one of the things that can come neither too late nor too early."

• English lawyer, philosopher and economist, influential representative of reforms • studies of law at Oxford • from 1772 a lawyer • considerable support for the codification of English law - placing stress on the principle of benefit as the main principle of legislation • founder of utilitarianism • fighter against colonialism (freeman of revolutionary France) •

His "Plan for general and everlasting peace" among nations was only published fifty years after he wrote it. England and France served him as good examples; he reasoned that solving the problems of these two rivals might open the way to a similar solution of other European questions. He started from the principles of national modesty and a general interest in peace. In fourteen articles, he suggested the abolition of colonialism, of power agreements, of all business preferences, of excessive armed forces (their numbers should be stipulated by an international agreement), and of illegal diplomacy.

A unified Europe should have its own Congress or an Assembly of the Empire. To solve disputes among nations, he suggested the foundation of a common law court. He also considered the fact that each state should provide some quota of powers to put through the court decisions, but at the same time he supposed that this would not be necessary, as the free press would ensure such publicity for a verdict that it would be impossible not to respect it. But he also became aware of the danger of the press acting in the services of national egoism. He advocated attracting the common people to the unification of Europe by cutting down taxes.

Hlavní směry právní a státní filosofie [Main Directions of Legal and State Philosophy]. Praha 1885.
Grundsätze für ein künftiges Völkerrecht und einen dauernden Frieden. Halle 1915.
The Theory of Legislation. Littleton 1931.
An Introduction to the Principles of Morals and Legislation. New York 1948.
Utilitarianism. Oxford 2002.

BLUNTSCHLI JOHANN KASPAR

* 1808 Zurich   † 1881 Karlsruhe

"In its area Switzerland made clear and realized ideas and principles which are blessed and fruitful for all European state systems, which are assigned to ensure also peace in Europe. ... If this ideal is realized at some time in the future, then the international Swiss nationality can be incorporated into a larger Eropean community. ... If the great problem of a constitution for the European community of states is to be solved, then careful preservation of the independence and freedom of the united nations is an absolute vital condition for it."

• Swiss liberal politician, lawyer, and political scientist • from 1833 work for Zürich University • 1848-1861 Professor at Munich and Heidelberg Universities • 1861-1871 Member of Parliament • significant contribution to the formulation of international military law •

In 1878 he published a paper on "The Organization of the European Confederacy of States", in which he tried to shift the issues of the concept of federalism and confederalism from the level of general proclamations to the level of practical policy. In doing this he was able to start from his own experience as a Swiss citizen. Especially when dealing with the issue of nationalism, he pointed to the inspiring Swiss example of "the nationalities with an international character". Even though he attributed an important role in the unification of Europe to Switzerland, he did not do so to the same extent as did Mazzini in Italy or Hugo in France and he doubted whether the European states could ever imitate the Swiss system of cantons since he was not able to find enough good will in them to sacrifice something of their own sovereignty. According to his suggestion, at the head of the confederated Europe there should be a Federal Council comprising representatives of all the states, whose decisions would be subject to the approval of the Senate, which would be elected by the people. He took into account the leading role of the great powers in the Federal Council. Trying to make the European confederation acceptable for all the states, he consistently stressed the fact that the Council and the Senate would only be competent in the fundamental issues of European politics, such as the existence and safety of states and questions of war and peace, etc.

Geschichte des Allgemeinen Staatsrechts und der Politik. München 1867.
Allgemeines Staatsrecht. München 1868.
Das moderne Kriegsrecht der zivilisierten Staaten. Nördlingen 1874.
International Law. Beijing 1880.
Gesammelte kleine Schriften. Nördlingen 1881.
The Theory of the Modern State. Oxford 1885.
Die schweizerische Nationalität. Zürich 1915.
The Theory of the State. Oxford 1921.
Die Organisation des europäischen Staatenvereines. Darmstadt 1962.
Geschichte der neueren Staatswissenschaft: allgemeines Staatsrecht und Politik seit dem 16. Jahrhundert bis zur Gegenwart. Aalen 1990.

BONAPARTE NAPOLEON

* 1769 Ajaccio † 1821 St. Helena

"The peace at Moscow ended my war activities. The great world issue was ensured against any accident and a period of stability began. A new horizon appeared, new work was called for, everything for the well-being of all. The European system had been founded; what had to be solved was how to organize it."

• French general and politician • 1778 arrival in France • 1779-1784 scholarship student at the military school in Brienne • 1784 military school in Paris - specialization in artillery • 1785 sub-lieutenant in the French army • supporter of the Great French Revolution and defender of the Republic • 1793 liberator of besieged Toulon - promoted to Brigadier-General • partner in the Directory • 1796 Italian campaign - the first victory over the Austrians • 1798-1799 Egyptian expedition • 1799 First Consul, gradual introduction of dictatorship • 1800-1801 reorganization of the state administration and build-up of the army • 1802 life Consul • 1804 coronation as the French Emperor • 1805 new wave of French expansion in Europe • gradual growth of power and extension of his sphere of influence • 1812 defeat in Russia • 1814 abdication after the defeat at Leipzig, exile to Elba • 1815 "Hundred Days" - defeat at Waterloo • final loss of the throne - deportation to St. Helena •

Napoleon's era brought about the disruption of a series of attempts to achieve a European balance and it brought about the introduction of a policy of one dominant power - France - which would dictate the situation in Europe. The Marquis de Laplace, the mastermind behind the introduction of the decimal system and simplification of the measuring system, praised "Napoleon the Great" because, due to his direct rule over one half of Europe and indirect control of the other, the same legal and measuring systems could soon be applied throughout Europe. At that time, a number of other European thinkers had worked on formulating grandiose projects for a European republic or a European monarchy, as a result of Napoleon's development from a Consul into an Emperor. Napoleon himself dreamed of world supremacy, but after the defeat in Egypt, he had to limit his ambition to Europe, a continent about which he once stated contemptuously: "This old Europe bores me."

Recapitulating his plans for Europe in his second exile on St. Helena, he declared that the victors at Waterloo stole his ideas from him as he, too, had been heading towards a European Congress and a Holy Alliance. He wanted to finish with wars as soon as Russia was conquered and turn to working for European prosperity - pushing through an "All Sovereigns' Alliance" in which every problem was to be solved in a "family circle". A European association of states would have had a common code of laws, a law court, a common currency, a unified system of measurement units, free passage for vessels on rivers and the seas, minimum military forces (namely sovereigns' guards only), etc. In this way, it would have been possible to establish one nation in Europe, which would have become a homeland for everybody.

These grand ideas only disguised the harsh reality of the military domination of Europe by the French army and the Emperor's dictatorship, which, to a great extent, worked against the progressive effect of Napoleon's destruction of the obsolete feudal structures of Europe.

Discours. Paris 1813.
Opinions of Napoleon the First on Russia and Poland Expressed at St. Helena. London 1855.
Lettres inédites de Napoléon Ier (an VIII-1815). Paris 1897.
Memoirs of the Emperor Napoleon. London 1901.
Briefe Napoleons des ersten in drei banden. Stuttgart 1909-1910.
Memoirs of Napoleon Bonaparte, the Court of the First Empire. New York 1910.

Válečné proklamace [War Proclamations]. Praha 1913.

Napoleonovy paměti [Napoleon's Memoirs]. Praha 1929.

Napoleon jako myslitel, vojevůdce, státník, národohospodář, hlava rodiny a člověk ve svých projevech [Napoleon as a Thinker, Commander, Statesman, Economist, Head of the Family, and Man in his Speeches]. Praha 1936.

Císař a člověk. Z Napoleonovy korespondence [An Emperor and Man. From Napoleon's Correspondence]. Brno 1937.

Lettres personnelles des souverains à l'empereur Napoléon Ier. Paris 1939.

Ich, der Kaiser: eine Autobiographie. München 1978.

BRIAND ARISTIDE

* 1862 Nantes   † 1932 Paris

"In my opinion, there must exist a kind of federative bond among the nations whose geographical location corresponds with that of the nations of Europe. ... That is the kind of union I would like to create. It is clear that this unification can be applied first of all in the economic field: it is the most pressing problem. I believe that it is possible to achieve good results. But I am also sure that - seen from the political and social points of view - a federative union, which will keep the sovereignty of the participating nations untouched, can be useful."

• French politician and diplomat • excellent lawyer and outstanding speaker • studies of law at Paris and Nantes Universities • a lawyer by profession - from 1893 in Paris • member and from 1901 Secretary of the Socialist Party • 1902 elected Member of Parliament • 1906 member of the Government for the first time - Minister of Public Education and Culture • in the following governments often the Minister of Foreign Affairs • 1909-1911 Prime Minister (by 1931 ten times) • after World War I supporter of activities of the League of Nations • initiator of disarmament efforts • 1925 promoter of conciliation with Germany - signatory of the Locarno Agreement • 1928 co-author of the "Briand - Kellog Pact" • 1930 plan for a European Federation • 1926 the Nobel Prize for Peace •

He belonged among those French politicians who realized that Europe could not be integrated by French hegemonism and that his country, too, needed fixed links all over Europe. As early as before World War I, he was a well-known pacifist and he advocated uniform international solutions of questions concerning education and school systems. As the Minister of Foreign Affairs and the Prime Minister, he repeatedly proclaimed the necessity for a European federation. A historic conciliation of the French and the Germans was to be its basis. He aroused responses to this idea in the League of Nations and was asked to further clarify his ideas. His closest collaborator, Alexis Saint-Léger (as a poet he was awarded the Nobel Prize under the pseudonym of Saint-John Perse), wrote in 1930 his "Memorandum on the Organization of the System of the European Union of Nations", based on Briand's perception. It required the creation of a whole European structure - an assembly of representatives of all states, a political board, European law court, European secretariat, etc. But all that did not appear to be realistic as such, when, at the same time, the absolute sovereignty of all member countries was proclaimed. Nevertheless, Briand's plan was, after a long period of time, a project which managed to bridge the gulf between the world of powerless Utopian idealists and the world of those in power, who wanted to use it to realistically push through the ideas of the idealists. Since at that time nationalism was, once again, on the rise and Hitler had formulated his monstrous vision of a unified Europe, Briand's plan stood no chance whatsoever. World War II was a cruel mockery of the already mentioned "Briand - Kellog Pact", which had been accepted almost unanimously, and by which states effectively decided to abandon war as an instrument of policy.

La Séparation des Églises et de l'État. Paris 1909.
Memorandum über die Organisation eines europäischen Bundessystems.
    In: Paneuropa, Jg. 6, 1930.
Union federale européenne. 1930.

BURCKHARDT JACOB CHRISTOPH

* 1818 Basel   † 1897 Basel

"For Europe only one single thing has always been a death blow: crushing mechanical power, whether it started from a barbarian nation lusting for conquest or from the accumulated domestic means of power of a state, or in the service of a tendency, e.g. the masses of our days. ... A saviour of Europe is, first of all, he who will protect it from the danger of a forced political, religious, and social unity and forced levelling which threatens its specific quality, namely the multiple richness of its spirit."

• Swiss philosopher and cultural historian • studies of philosphy and history at Berlin University • disciple of the founder of the German positivist historic school, L. Rank • 1855-1858 Professor at Zürich University, from 1858 in Basel • admirer of and expert on ancient Greece and the Italian Renaissance • proclaimer of individualism as a permanently valid ideal of man •

He was a historian of Europe, and Nietzsche unconditionally admired him as a teacher. For Burckhardt the links which held our continent together were the institution of the Papacy, the Holy Roman Empire, overseas discoveries, a number of great personalities, and the permanent resistance of nations against the hegemony of a great power. In the history of Europe he appreciated the spiritual richness, culture, diversity, and liberal individualism. Although, when searching through the past, he was able to find the permanently rising advancement of Europe, its prospects did not appear very optimistic to him. He was especially afraid of national, political, and social tensions and of military dictatorships destroying democracy and making an overall "shutting - up" obligatory.

The clairvoyance of this humanist, who scientifically researched the culture of the Renaissance and focused on those parts of world history which had an influence on European culture, signified in a prophetic way a considerable amount of the troubled future of Europe.

Briefe an F. von Preen. Stuttgart - Berlin 1922.
Historische Fragmente. Basel 1942.
Europa: Bilder seiner Landschaft und Kultur. Zürich 1952.
Sullys Plan einer Europaordnung. Hamburg 1952.
Úvahy o světových dějinách [Reflections on World History]. Praha 1971.

BURKE EDMUND

* 1729 Dublin   † 1797 London

"As far as war, a means of evil and violence, is concerned, it can be taken as the only instrument of justice among nations. It cannot be eradicated from any country in the world. Do not those who claim otherwise mislead themselves with the intention of misleading us? But the most significant aim of human wisdom is at least to reduce evil, if we are not able to do away with it."

• British politician, writer, philosopher, and aesthetician • after arrival in London, outstanding representative and ideologist of the Whig Party • from 1765 member of the House of Commons • excellent speaker and organizer • critic of absolutist tendencies of George III, slavery in colonies, oppression in Ireland, and anti-American customs policy • opponent of the French Revolution - supporter of English participation in the anti-French coalition •

This "English Cicero", a defender of the rights of America and one of the first opponents of the Jacobin ideology, took Montesquieu as the source of his ideas and inspired Gentz. It was only in the 20th century that his voice, very little listened to in his day, was paid attention to and later became very popular with the neo-Conservatives, especially for its strong sense of truthfulness and policy of the balance of powers. Like Gentz, he believed that wars were inevitable but in no sense did he praise them. He was strongly in favour of the balance of power in Europe and looked for a way between Christian ideals and national realities, between the need for European unity and national interests.

Letters on the Proposal for Peace with the Regicide Directory of France. Oxford 1874-1878.

Burke's Politics; Selected Writings and Speeches on Reform, Revolution and War. New York 1959.

The Philosophy of Edmund Burke. A Selection from his Speeches and Writings. Ann Arbor 1960.

A Complete History of the Late War or Annual Register, of its Rise, Progress, and Events, in Europe, Asia, Africa and America. Dublin 1983.

CATTANEO CARLO

* 1801 Milan   † 1869 Castagnola

"If there is a unifying element in Europe, which certainly had its roots in Asia..., then there certainly is also a separating element, which is the principle of different nationalities. ... The various combinations between the trend towards unity and the long-established variety have not come from Asia but have happened, have been realized on the continent of Europe."

• Italian politician, economist, historian, dramatist, and poet • studies of philology and philosophy • teacher of grammar and rhetoric at a grammar school in Milan • 1839 founder of the "Politecnico" magazine • in 1848, in spite of his reservations about the state of readiness of the uprising, active participant in the Revolution • participation in the defence of Milan • departure for Switzerland after Austrian victory • 1859 return to Italy • elected Member of Parliament • representative of the Republican opposition • critic of the situation in Italy •

Along with Hugo, it was he who is supposed to have been the first to use the expression "The United States of Europe". His conception of unification was federalistic. He found the tension between uniformity and diversity inevitable, and so he recognized the necessity for basic "uniforming" elements, but at the same time advocated no loss of identity of the unified nations. He rejected romantic illusions about a new golden age of Europe and he connected his belief in its irrevocable integration with the progress of civilization, with the historic experience of nations, and with economic necessities. His attitude towards the problems of unification was one of a researcher, a scientist. From this basis he reached a firm conviction about the inevitability of the unification of Italy and, later on, of the whole Continent as well.

Notizie naturali e civili sulla Lombardia. Firenze 1888.
Scritti politici ed epistolario. Firenze 1892-1901.
L'insurrezione di Milano e le Considerazioni sul 1848. Torino 1949.

CHAADAYEV PETR YAKOVLEVITCH

*1794 Moscow   † 1856 Moscow

"Standing alone in this world, we brought nothing to it, we have not taught it anything, we have not added any thought to the body of human ideas, in no way have we taken part in the progress of human reason, and everything that reached us from this progress has been distorted. ... It is not necessary to run after others, but to evaluate ourselves in the right way and to judge what we are like in order to be able to wade out of lies and achieve the truth. Then we will be able not only to proceed forward, but to walk faster than others, since we came  *after them, we have got all their experience and the works of the past centuries. ... The day will come when we take a stand in the middle of spiritual Europe. ... That will be the result, a logical result of our long-lasting loneliness - all great things have come from a desert."*

• Russian thinker and writer • studies at Moscow University • 1812-1814 officer in the Tsarist army in the war against Napoleon • after 1814 the Tsar's adjutant • 1823-1826 stay abroad, cooperation with Schelling • 1826 return to Russia • arrest for his contacts with the Decembrists - release for lack of evidence • under police surveillance for the rest of his life • 1836 one of his "Philosophical Papers" published in a magazine • outrage in the monarchist walks of society • new persecution, claimed insane • in the '40s participant in the disputes of the "zapadniks" with the Slavophiles • 1848 author of a leaflet giving information on revolutions in Europe •

In his personality Europeanism both fought with and was bound to Slavophilia. In his "Philosophical Papers" (written in French) his attitude towards the history of Russia was extremely critical and negative. (N. Berd'ajev said of Chaadayev that he "denies the history of his own country".) When the csar proclaimed him an insane person, he wrote his "Apologetics of a Madman", in which a faith in the messianistic mission of the Russian nation was added to his condemnation of the past of Russia.

He came to his European attitude on the basis of his conviction that all European nations have "the same physiognomy and physiology" and that there exist mutual bonds among them, Christianity above all. He recognized that each nation also has something special, but it is by combining all the individualities that the basic common ideas, first of all ideas of duty, justice, and law and order can come into existence. Although Russia has not given anything to Europe and is not a part of it, because it was pushed away after Peter the Great's leaving, it will nevertheless be nobody else but Russia that will save and unify Europe.

Filozofické listy. - Apologie bláznova [Philosophical Papers.
    Apologetics of a Madman]. Praha 1987.
Statji i pisma [Articles and Letters]. Moskva 1987.

Churchill Winston Leonard Spencer

* 1874 Blenheim Palace † 1965 London

"Winners are absorbed within a noise of disharmonic voices, losers are lost in a dark silence of despair. Without the generosity of the United States, that clearly understood that the decay or damnation of Europe will also pull their fates into common misery, the return of the Middle Ages, with all their barbarism and filth, would be inevitable. And this can happen again at any time! Nevertheless, there is a device that may, if used generally and spontaneously, miraculously change the whole scene and in a few years make all of Europe as free and happy as Switzerland is now. What is this most effective device? It is the restoration of the European family...; we must create an order that will make possible life in peace, safety, and freedom. We must establish something like the United States of Europe. Only then can hundreds of millions of hard-working people regain the common joys and hopes that make life worth living."

• British statesman, strong-willed politician, unstinting supporter of parliamentarianism, far-sighted pragmatist • representative of the Conservative Party • 1895-1900 career in the army, fighting in Cuba, India, and South Africa • 1900 elected to the House of Commons for the first time • from 1908 member of the Government • 1924-1929 Chancellor of the Exchequer • 1932-1939 denouncer of appeasement - 1938 opponent of "The Munich Agreement" • from 1940 the Prime Minister of the British Government • organizer and representative of the anti-fascist coalition • 1941 signing the "Atlantic Charter" • 1945 Yalta negotiations • 1945 resignation after the Labour election victory • 5th March 1946 speech at Fulton University - the term "Iron Curtain" used for the first time • 1951 return to the Prime Minister's office • 1953 the Nobel Prize for Literature • 1953 knighted • 1955 resignation in favour of A. Eden •

The failure of European policy made him, more than others, responsible for leading the fight against the total destruction of democracy and humanism in Europe. World War II made the issue of European understanding even more urgent than WWI did. Therefore, Churchill was one of the initiators of the "Atlantic Charter", which formulated the principles of the peaceful cooperation of nations after the war. Churchill also heard about the declaration of the European Resistance Movement (nine states, including the CSR) issued in Geneva in 1944, which expressed the conviction that after its liberation from fascism Europe could be made permanently safe against further tragedies only in the form of a federal union. His appeal to European nations to create "the United Nations of Europe", delivered on 16th September 1946 in Zürich, was a crucial stimulus in the one-hundred-year effort for European integration.

Undoubtedly, his proposal only summarized ideas written and pronounced by hundreds of thinkers before, but this time, it was not possible to overlook or forget it. Within a few years, Churchill's words started to come true.

A United Europe: One Way to Stop a New War. London 1946.
Vereinigte Staaten von Europa. Zürich 1946.
Europa der Gegenwart. Wien 1947.
Nelítostný zápas [Merciless Fight]. Praha 1947.
Červánky osvobození [A Herald of Liberation]. Praha 1948.
Europe United. Boston 1950.
The European Spirit. London 1979.
Triumph and Tragedy. Boston 1985.
Druhá světová válka [World War II]. Praha 1992-1993.

CLOOTS JEAN - BAPTISTE

* 1755 Cleve † 1794 Paris

"The body does not fight against itself and the human race will live in peace if it is one body, one nation. ... Paris will be the linking point, the vanguard of the world-wide community."

• French politician of Prussian origin • 1776 emigration to Paris • collaboration on the "Encyclopaedia" • admirer of the French Enlightenment • in 1789 keen supporter of the French Revolution • 1792 member of the Convention • originally Girondist, later supporter of the radical Jacobin movement • advocate of war as a means of spreading revolution in Europe • 1793 foremost activist in the movement for doing away with religion • 1794 branded as a foreign agent • death sentence and execution in the trial of the Héberts •

His formulation of the ideal of the first stage of the French Revolution was the most telling of all - an ideal of a world-wide brotherhood of people. All Europe was to be liberated and unified in the spirit of the Enlightenment. The wars which had to be fought so that people could realize this aim were to be the last ones in history. But before long even Cloots' way of thinking started to be controlled by his conviction that France, as the bringer of liberty and happiness to Europe, should have a special position and every war it was going to wage would be a holy one. That was why he took the principle as a reactionary one. On April 21 1792 he handed over his memorial publication "The World Republic" to the Convention. In it, he called for all governments to be done away with and replaced by one centralized government. As his life also finished in a revolutionary place of execution, he was not able to follow, during the further stages of the revolution, how the principle of federalism became condemned and the ideal of a free Europe was completely overshadowed by French national hegemonism.

L'orateur du genre humain ou Dépęche du Prussien, Cloots au Prussien Hertzberg. Paris 1791.
La république universelle, ou Adresse aux tyrannicides. Paris 1793.
L'orateur du genre humain, la République Universelle. Paris 1793.

COMTE ISIDORE AUGUSTE

* 1798 Montpellier   † 1857 Paris

"Our historic research will then have to be restricted exclusively to the élite and the vanguard of mankind, which consists of a large part of the white race or of European nations, but first of all we have - to be exact - to concentrate on the modern epochs, on the nations of Western Europe... ."

• French philosopher and sociologist • graduate from the lyceum in his native town • studies at the École Polytechnique in Paris • from 1817 disciple, secretary, and collaborator of Saint-Simon • teacher of mathematics at the Polytechnique in Paris • 1830-1842 work on a six-volume publication "A Course of Positive Philosophy" - explanations of three stages of historic development • 1833 dismissal from job as a teacher - struggles along, supported by his backers and disciples •

The favourite disciple and later opponent of Saint-Simon, a founder of modern sociology, after the fashion of his teacher he became a convinced and mystic supporter of "Eurocentrism". According to his conviction, Europe had played the most important part in the history of mankind. Europe's mission is to unite the whole world after it has been united itself.

Of course, he concentrated his social analyses on the society in which social development went furthest and which he considered the most perfect, i.e. the European. The development of Comte's thoughts unfortunately reached absurdity - he mixed positive science with a religion in which scientists are priests. Later on he became completely enthralled by mysticism.

Projet d'une organisation politique pour l'Europe, avant pour objet de procurer aux souverains et aux peuples une paix générale et perpétuelle. Hambourg 1818.
Cours de Philosophie Positive. Paris 1894.
Sociologie [Sociology]. Praha 1927.
Rozumová anarchie a sociální zla [Anarchy of Reason and Social Evils]. Praha 1946.

CONDORCET MARIE JEAN ANTOINE DE

* 1743 Ribemont   † 1794 Bourg-la Reine

"If we have a look at the current situation of the globe, first of all we will make ourselves sure that in Europe all enlightened people have adopted the principles of the French constitution already. We will see that they are announced and spread so loudly that the endeavours of monarchs and priests cannot prevent them from penetrating into the straw huts of slaves. ... Have a look at the history of our enterprise, our settlements in Africa or in Asia: you will see our trade monopolies, our betrayals, our blood contempt of people of another colour or faith. ... But the moment is coming, undoubtedly, the moment when we are not seen as destroyers or tyrants, when we are useful instruments or broad-minded liberators. Then Europeans will be - by restricting themselves to free trade - too much informed by their rights to despise the rights of other nations, they will respect the independence which they have hurt so disdainfully until today."

• French philosopher, economist, and politician • supporter of Voltaire and friend of d'Alembert • collaborator on the "Encyclopaedia" - author of the sections on issues from the field of economics • first publisher of collected works of Voltaire • 1789 participant in the Revolution - a member of the Legislative Assembly (1791 its Chairman) • 1792 submitter of a proposal for organizing the public system of education to the Legislative Assembly • 1792 member of the Convention

• author of the proposal for the French Constitution • 1794 arrest together with the Girondists • his death in prison (murder or suicide) •

In his opinions can be found a clear reflection of the ideals of the Great French Revolution, a victim of which he paradoxically became (as did many of its other proponents). In his work "An Outline of a Historical Picture of the Progress of the Human Spirit" he proclaimed especially international scientific collaboration and the development of culture and education all over the world as well as the necessity for people to possess social security. He was a critic of European colonizing activities and he realized not only the damage they brought to the inhabitants of the conquered areas on other continents but also the negative consequences of colonialism - becoming accustomed to humiliation and "terrorizing" - for the spiritual situation in Europe. Nevertheless he believed that there were so many enlightened heads in Europe that the ideas of human liberty, equality, and brotherhood were bound to win not only here but on all continents. And so he belonged among the sort of Europeans whose considerations exceeded the European dimension.

Náčrt historického obrazu pokroků lidského ducha [An Outline of a Historical Picture of the Progress of the Human Spirit]. Praha 1968.
Arithmétique politique: textes rares ou inédits (1767-1789). Paris 1994.
Reflections on the English Revolution of 1688, and that of the French, August 10, 1792. London 1792.
The Political Theory of Condorcet. Oxford 1991.
Cinq mémoires sur l'instruction publique. Paris 1994.
Vie de Voltaire. Paris 1994.

CONSTANT REBEQUE HENRI BENJAMIN DE

* 1767 Lausanne   † 1830 Paris

"It is worth noticing that invariability was not accepted anywhere as positively as during the Revolution which came in the name of human rights and freedom. While love for the homeland has its roots in purely being fond of local interests, manners and customs, our patriots declared war on all of those things. They let the natural spring of love for the homeland dry up. ... The situation was not far from their identifying towns and provinces with numbers - in the same way as they identified their legions and army corps. ... Attachment to local customs is connected with all unselfish, noble, and pious feelings. How regrettable is the policy which makes an uprising of it! ... Variety means organization, uniformity mechanization. Variety is life, uniformity is death. ... That is why it is our aim to create a large federative state system in Europe which should serve progress and correspond to the spirit of the century."

• French politician, journalist, and writer (from a Swiss Huguenot family) • 1794 arrival in revolutionary France • liberal, supporter of the constitutional monarchy • 1795-1799 collaborator of the Directory • critic of Napoleon's regime • 1803-1813 exile • 1816 return to Paris - during the Restoration of the Bourbons member of the liberal opposition •

He was a propagator of European political liberalism. He categorically rejected the Jacobin ideal of a centralized European nation, as well as Napoleon's way of unifying the Continent by means of force (in his famous polemic "De l'Esprit de Conquéte et de l'Usurpation dans leurs rapports avec la Civilisation européenne"). His plan for a European union originated in the negation of wars among nations as well as in their unification into uniformity. In a united Europe he did not intend to deprive nations of their individuality; on the contrary, he emphasized the qualities which are brought about by variety in the lives of nations and in the exchange of their fruits. He rejected the role of an omnipotent state and contrasted it to a return to independent localities of citizens on which the system of European unification should be based in peaceful ways. We can see in him one of the predecessors of the present-day federalists who want to keep all the positive features of various national kinds of culture, even in a united Europe.

Acte Additionnel aux Constitutions de l'Empire. Paris 1814.
Über die Gewalt. Stuttgart 1948.

COUDENHOVE-KALERGI RICHARD NICOLAUS VON

* 1894 Tokyo   † 1972 Schruns

"Ladies and gentlemen of Europe! The hour of Europe's fate has struck! Every day in European factories there are forged weapons to tear apart European men, in European laboratories there are fermented poisons to kill European women and children. In the meantime, Europe, incomprehensibly heedless, flies in the face of Providence. ... The only salvation ... is: pan-Europe; joining all the democratic states of continental Europe into an international group, into a political and economic purpose-made union. ... If the states of Europe want it - pan-Europe will come into existence: it is  *only necessary to withdraw one's voice from support for all the candidates and parties whose programme is anti-European. ... A simple truth has to be repeated again and again: a divided and fragmented Europe is conducive to war, oppression, and poverty, a united Europe to peace and well-being! ... Save Europe and your children!"*

• Austrian politician, political scientist, and journalist • from a cultured cosmopolitan family • youth with Czech-German background at the Mansion of Poběžovice • studies of philosophy and history at Vienna University • interest in journalism • 1923 his work "Pan-Europe" - basis of Pan-European Movement • 1924 first number of the "Pan-Europe" magazine • in 1938 leaves Austria after the "Anschluss" • short stay in Bratislava • emigration to Switzerland, later to the USA • 1940-1946 Professor of History at a University in New York • 1944 proposal for

COUDENHOVE-KALERGI RICHARD NICOLAUS VON

"The United States of Europe" • from 1947 General Secretary of the European Parliamentary Union • 1950 the Charles Prize • 1952-1965 Honorary President of the Council of Europe •

He represents quite a new chapter in the history of Europeanism, which was opened after World War I. After numerous previous projects and considerations of European unification, Earl Coudenhove-Kalergi not only came with a new plan, but he dedicated all his life to activities aimed at its realization. Traditions in his family, his Austrian - Greek - Japanese blood, and the background in which he grew up formed him in a completely supranational way. He flatly rejected nationalism, anti-Semitism, Nazism, and Bolshevism as a matter of principle. He could see the salvation of Europe from further catastrophes in a voluntary federative union - in "Pan-Europe", in the United States of Europe. He did not take into consideration either Russia or England. He was rather skeptical regarding the League of Nations and he tried to spread the ideas of peace and cooperation in Europe and to get support from the general public as well as from renowned politicians by the promotional and organizational activities of the "Pan-European Union", a movement which he himself established (a "sun cross" was its symbol - a red cross in a golden sun, a sign of humanity and reason) and by the "Pan-Europe" magazine as well. He found the most positive response in Austria, Czechoslovakia, and France. He organized several pan-European congresses and intended to create a "European nation". A lot of his ideas were identical with those of Otto von Habsburg. In 1946 he helped Winston Churchill to draft his memorable speech, later taken as a direct impulse towards a realistic unification of the continent. (He could see the personification of a European in ancient Ulysses, who bore - in the 20th century - a resemblance to nobody else but W. Churchill.) In 1947 he founded a European Parliamentary Union, which laid the foundation of European parliamentarism, and he took part in establishing the European institutions and organizations by means of which the dream of a united Europe achieved a palpable form in its Western part. His efforts to reconcile pan-Europeans to Ch. de Gaulle's policy met a lack of understanding and Coudenhove responded to it in 1965 by resigning from the office of the Honorary President of the European

Movement. He spent the rest of his life in seclusion but he was able to observe how the work to which he had contributed more than anybody else was growing unstoppably, even though it faced difficulties.

Gebote des Lebens. Leipzig 1931.
Kommen die Vereinigten Staaten von Europa. Leipzig 1938.
Kampf um Europa. Aus meinem Leben. Zürich 1949.
Die europäische Nation. Stuttgart 1953.
Totaler Mensch, totaler Staat. Wien 1965.
Ein Leben für Europa. Köln 1966.
Weltmacht Europa. Stuttgart 1971.
Pan-Evropa [Pan-Europe]. Praha 1993.
Pan-Europe. Geneve 1997.

CRUCÉ EMERIC

* 1590   † 1648

"We should admit to ourselves that human society forms one body, the parts of which are connected with one another: ailments of one part of the body always afflict the other parts. ... What a joy it would be if people could move freely everywhere, understand one another without any problems with borders of countries, without any formalities, as if all earth were (as it really should be) one town created for everybody. ... I can only contribute to this by my wishes and modest vision. Nevertheless, I have wanted to leave this testimony to my descendants. If it were useless, all right: paper and words do not cost much. In this case I declare, along with Solón, that I have said and done my best for the well-being of everybody."

• French writer • monk, teacher at a school in Paris (called the "little Parisian teacher") • 1623 publication "New Cyneas" (called after a wise and eloquent man sent to Rome by King Pyrrhus to discuss peace) •

His vision of the world resulted in a complete rejection of war, which - monarchs should also realize - shakes even thrones. In his considerations he reached over the boundaries of Europe and he asked for peace not only for this continent but for the whole world, because he could see people like him everywhere, he could see nations connected by natural and unbreakable bonds everywhere. He naturally developed his national tolerance into a religious policy of appeasement as well. He could see the best way of preventing war in a court, to the authority of which the sides in a war would always submit. At the same time he suggested setting up a General Assembly (a Senate), consisting of the envoys of all monarchs, to settle international problems; he proposed Venice, a neutral and geographically acceptable place for all sides, as the seat of this body. Out of all rulers he emphasized the roles of the Pope and the Turkish Sultan (!). He believed that the Senate would be able to find means how to bring everybody to their senses. He also thought about what nations were going to do when their energy would no longer be discharged in wars; he proposed fostering education and the sciences, the development of trade, and great projects to make rivers navigable, to gain more land, and to improve roads and transport. He also recommended the unification of weights and measures and he was brought into ecstasy by the dream of the free movement of people and goods.

Der neue Kineas. In: K. von Raumer, Ewiger Friede. Freiburg 1953.
The New Cineas. New York 1972.
Le Nouveau Cynée: ou discours des occasions et moyens d'établir une paix générale et la liberté du commerce pour tout le monde. Paris 1976.

DANTE ALIGHIERI

* 1265 Florence   † 1321 Ravenna

"It is obvious that general peace is the best among the things that lead to our eternal bliss... . And therefore it is clear that for the happiness and prosperity of the world it is necessary to have only one monarchy or one empire... ."

• outstanding Italian poet • orphan from 1277 • studies of theology and philosophy in Florence • supporter of the White Guelfs' Party • from 1295 high political functions in Florence • 1298 participant in fights against Arezzo and Pisa • 1301 ambassador in Rome • after the victory of the Black Guelfs sentenced (in absentia) to exile first, afterwards to death • exile - Verona, Bologna, Ravenna • for the rest of his life vain efforts to be allowed back to Florence • endeavour to gain the favour of the influential inhabitants of Florence by his philosophical publication "Convivio" (digest of the knowledge of the 13th century) • 1306-1320 work on his magnificent piece of work "Commedia" •

He expressed his vision of the political arrangement of Europe (and the rest of the world) first of all in his publication "On Monarchy", published shortly after the rise of the plan of P. du Bois, a contemporary of his. His vision is not always quite clear and its determinism, shaped by the situation in divided Italy, is obvious. On the one side he emphasized Christian unity in the sense of the Christian myth of the Middle Ages, but on the other he demanded the separation of secular power from the clerical. He took a federalistic union of nations under Roman patronage as his basic idea. According to him, the Pope was the decisive authority from whom even the power of the Emperor, who was to guarantee order in Europe, was derived. The peaceful stability of the Continent, which was the chief value for Dante, could be ensured only by a universal monarchy, which was not expected to deprive the individual states of the European union of their own identities.

Dante a Češi [Dante and the Czechs]. Olomouc 1921.
Die Monarchie. Breslau 1926.
O jediné vládě [On the Only Government]. Praha 1942.
Nový život [New Life]. Praha 1965.
Božská komedie [A Divine Comedy]. Praha 1984.

DAWSON CHRISTOPHER

* 1889 Harlington Hall   † 1970 Midhurst

"Many a great 19th-century historian was also an apostle of the cult of nationalism and books on history were often booklets of narrow-minded national propaganda... . All the social life of Europe was usually undermined and falsified by this fact. The World War was a great avenger of this mistake. ... The danger of nationalism is not based on its devotion to the traditions of the past or on its defence of national unity and the right to self-determination; it is giving this unity parity of treatment with ... the supranational unity of culture ... which is false. Unfortunately, nobody is particular about defending the issue of Europe. Every individual nation creates thousands of inalienable rights to defend itself. ... But if our European culture is to stay alive, it is necessary to bring back to life general European awareness and the sense of its historic unity. We need not worry that this will increase hostility between Europe and non-European cultures. ... If a real world culture should ever come into existence, then it will be only in the way of increasing mutual understanding and not through the fact that historic traditions will be simply neglected."

• English historian, philosopher, and sociologist • education at one of the oldest English schools, Winchester • studies at Oxford University • 1911 departure for Sweden - studies of national economics, history, and sociology • 1914 conversion to Catholicism • extensive scientific activities - about 230 philosophical and historical publications • from

DAWSON CHRISTOPHER

1930 senior lecturer at Liverpool University, later at Edinburgh University • 1958-1962 Professor at Harvard University • member of the British Academy •

He was one of the most enthusiastic defenders of cultural unity in Europe. That is why he devoted so much of his time to "the rise of Europe", i. e. the pre-national period of the history of Europe (e. g. in his book "The Creating of the West"); he recognized even the role of the so-called "barbarian" tribes in forming European culture and he also appreciated the mission of Constantine and Method and the personality of St. Adalbert. He rejected the evaluation of history by comparing it with the present day (as the apogee of history) but also the use of history "as a weapon against our time", for example for the benefit of national and religious propaganda. He argued with romantic, as well as with propagandistic, Catholic theories which separated medieval culture from reality. He warned against the idealization of the Middle Ages as an epoch of general faith and harmony which was said to have been broken by the Reformation. He did not categorically link the existence of Europe and its united spirit (as, for example, Novalis and his companions did) with Christianity or aristocratism, humanism, or the progress of science and technology at the last stage of its history, but at the same time he tried to understand these factors in their current as well as eternal importance. He stressed the need for spiritual and moral unity, also from the point of view of the growing confrontation with non-European races and cultures, while rejecting the theory of the superiority of European culture and its the right to dominate the world.

Die Wahre Einheit der europäischen Kultur. Eine geschichtliche Untersuchung. Regensburg 1935.
Pokrok a náboženství [Progress and Religion]. Praha 1947.
Europa. Idee und Wirklichkeit. München 1953.
The Making of Europe: an Introduction to the History of European Unity. Washington 1954.
The Dynamics of World History. New York 1956.
Understanding Europe. Fayetteville 1991.
Krize západní vzdělanosti [A Crisis of Western Education]. Praha 1992.

DAWSON CHRISTOPHER

Zrození Evropy [The Birth of Europe]. Praha 1994.
Porozumět Evropě. [Understanding Europe] Praha 1995.
Christianity and European Culture Selections from the Work of Christopher
    Dawson. Washington 1998.

DE GAULLE CHARLES ANDRÉ JOSEPH MARIE

* 1890 Lille † 1970 Colombey-les-Deux-Églises

"Active politics means a set of accepted decisions or accomplished deeds with the awareness of risks, and with the support of the people. The government of nations must be able and responsible for forming the politics. Naturally, we should not forget that one day the nations of this continent will become one, and that a European government will be founded for the people. However, it would be ridiculous to act as if this day has already come. ... In our opinion, i. e. in the opinion of the Frenchmen, it is a matter of Europe to be truly European. A European Europe means that she exists for itself; or - in other words - in the middle of the world; and that she has her own policies."

• French general and statesman • participant in WWI • 1921 senior lecturer in military history at Saint-Cyr • 1934 author of a document demanding the mechanization of the French army and equipping it with tanks • 1937 colonel • 1940 brigadier-general, commander of an armoured division fighting against the German invasion • departure from the country after the defeat of France • 18 June 1940 memorable radio appeal to continue fighting against the Nazis from the territory of the French colonies • 1944 at the head of the provisional French government • 1945 president of liberated France • 1946 withdrawal from public life • 1958 Minister of Defence, Prime Minister, and then President • 1962 credited with ending the war in Algeria • 1969 resignation after an unsuccessful referendum about state reforms proposed by him •

De Gaulle was a representative of the concept of "Europe de patries", i. e. a Europe consisting of individual nation states. He was against the strengthening of supranational structures. He fought hard to defend French national interests, through which he wanted to restore the international prestige of France. His aim was to make France into a dominant European power. The European Economic Community at that time served France for the protection of her own interests, especially in agriculture. De Gaulle did not hesitate to use this position to enforce French national interests, for instance using the "empty chair policy". This meant that France withdrew her representatives from the Council of Europe and thus blocked the work of this organ. De Gaulle perceived German-French relations as the cornerstone of European policy, especially in response to Anglo-Saxon influences. He tried to minimize the role of the USA in Europe, and especially in NATO. In 1966, France even left the military structures of NATO. De Gaulle also successfully blocked the integration of Great Britain into the European Community, because he did not want France to lose its position. He knew that Great Britain had even closer relations with the USA after WW II than ever before, and so he feared that the USA would use Great Britain as a means to engage in purely European matters. De Gaulle's European role was not always unambiguous, but he nevertheless markedly contributed to the strengthening of the European spirit.

L'Europe de l'Atlantique à l'Oural. Paris 1963.
Memoirs of Hope. New York 1971.
Memoiren der Hoffnung. Wien 1970-1971.
Lettres, notes et carnets 1945-1969. Paris 1984-1987.
Válečné paměti 1940-1944 [War memoirs 1940-1944]. Praha 1989.
Mémoires. Paris 2000.

DIEZ DEL CORRAL LUIS

* 1911 Logroño † 1998 Madrid

"The mission of Europe is far from finished, even though in some aspects of life it has retreated into the background and become smaller in significance... .

Europe has no choice other than to adapt to the new situation, forget about its former greatness, and try to look for a new vital force in its own heart. At the same time it must unite its strength, which hitherto has been dissipated in national diversities, so as to be able to compare favourably with new, young, and powerful protagonists. ...

But who could be more suited than Europe...? Nobody else's starting point is so rich and balanced as to integrate such a variety of areas of life, which, in the process of the expansion of the contemporary world, have evolved so differently; there is no-one else to maintain the old and imperishable treasure of classical and Christian humanism."

• Spanish historian and political thinker • in the '30s studies of history, law and political science in Madrid (where he was a follower of Ortega y Gasset), Berlin, and Fribourg • between 1936-1982 member of the Council of State • from 1947 Head of the Department of History and Political Science at Madrid University • member of three Royal Academies (history, political science, and fine arts) • 1966 - Director of the European Cultural Foundation in Amsterdam • 1980 Doctor Honoris Causae at the Sorbonne • 20 books and 200 scientific articles and papers • recipient of numerous prizes and awards (the French Order of the Legion d'Honneur, the Grand Cross of Alfonse X) •

In his "Rape of Europe" he frequently reacts to the thoughts of Toynbee by disagreeing with them. He saw European culture and civilization not only as penetrating the world and often harming it, but, many a time, in the modern era more than ever before, as being pillaged or even turned against its European creator. He was aware that the world, which, to a certain extent, the Europeans shaped, had now grown immensely bigger and was so strong that it could easily crush Europe. He admitted that Europe itself was partly responsible for a portion of its own unhappiness but he did not see its fate as being tragic (as opposed to, for instance, Spengler). On the contrary, he believed that the big decision which is to be made about Europe will be made in a spirit of heroism, enthusiasm, and an inability to give up. Thus, he did not view Europe as a sick man whose days have long been counted and who is only being prescribed medicines to enable him to enjoy what is left of his life. He believed that Europe's future was not without hope, partly because it was not for Europe's sake only but also concerned the rest of both the "robbed" and "robbing" world, whose own destiny is joined with Europe's. His thoughts culminate in the belief that Europe will not only survive but may end up playing a new world role in creating a humanism that will be more perfect since it will be enriched by great progress in science, technology, material abundance, and the social organization of human society.

El rapto de Europa. Madrid 1953.
Der Raub der Europa. München 1959.

Dostoevsky Fyodor Mihailovitch

* 1821 Moscow   † 1881 Petersburg

"It is possible to say - not only as a mere speculation but nearly with certainty - that Russia will appear as a stronger country than all the others in Europe in the near or even the very near future. ... Thus only one colossus will exist on the continent of Europe - Russia. It can happen in a much faster way than anticipated. The future of Europe lies with Russia. ... If necessary, we will draw our swords in the name of the oppressed and unhappy, even against our current interests. At the same time our belief that this is the real mission of Russia as such, its strength and its right, should grow stronger and stronger."

• Russian writer and thinker • cheerless childhood under the rule of his cruel father • graduate of a private grammar school in Moscow • 1837-1843 studies at military school in St. Petersburg • 1844 instead of a career as a civil servant swing to literature • 1849 arrest and death sentence for participation in the circle of M. V. Petrashevsky - verdict commuted to a ten-year stay in Siberia • 1850-1854 hard labour in Omsk • 1854-1859 military service in Semipalatinsk • 1859 pardoned and allowed to return to St. Petersburg and go on publishing books again • 1861-1867 rich short story and novel output, journalist and publishing activity (magazines "The Time" and "The Epoch") • 1862-1863 first journeys to western Europe - Paris, Geneva, London, Copenhagen, Rome • 1867 stay in Germany, Switzerland, and Italy • after return to

Russia publisher of the magazine "Dnjevnik pisatelja" [A Diary of a Writer] • 1871-1880 peak of his novel-writing activities •

His works are filled with European apocalyptic forecasts and, even more than with Chaadayev, with reflections on the position and the role of Russia. In them, the leading idea was the unique character of the role of the Russian Orthodox Church, which "had kept the divine face of Christ in its purity", which predetermined also the role of the Russian nation: to tell the whole of mankind the way they had lost. For Dostoevsky, the world meant, above all, Europe. He concluded that all European unifying efforts had ended in nothing but "a sad mirage" and therefore there was more hostility on the Continent than ever, everything was undermined and loaded with gun-powder, and just one spark would make for a cataclysmic tragedy. He forecast terrible torture and destruction ("Europe - a cemetery"). This is reflected also in some of his works - "The Devils", "Youth", and "The Brothers Karamazov". In its final hour Europe thus cannot but ask "Holy Russia" for help. The Russians may come and tame the enemies of Europe together with Count Bismarck and they themselves will become "the genuine Europeans", they will become the mightiest nation of their "second homeland". Europe has to become Russian so that Russia might become European.

Deník spisovatelův I, II [A Diary of a Writer I, II]. Praha 1910.
Zápisky z mrtvého domu [Notes from the House of the Dead]. Praha 1973.
Bratři Karamazovi [The Brothers Karamazov]. Praha 1980.
Petrohradská kronika [A Petersburg Cronicle]. Praha 1985.
Běsi [The Devils]. Praha 1987.
Zápisky z podzemí [Notes from the Underground]. Praha 1989.
A Writer's Diary. London 1995.
Une sale histoire. Arles 2002.

DU BOIS PIERRE

* around 1250   † after 1321

"When even sacredness and the teachings or prayers of the Holy Fathers did not bring an end to either military conflicts inside Christianity or all the dangers connected with them, how can the Pope believe that the preaching and teachings of contemporary or future administrators could finish the wars which they arose from? Stronger and more radical therapeutical remedies are demanded. It is necessary to establish criminal laws against war and to build Christian society on them."

• also known as Petrus de Bosco • French political thinker, lawyer (so-called legista), and writer • studies in Paris • from 1300 at the court of Philip IV, the Comely • support of the King's policy against Pope Boniface VIII • opponent of scholasticism of Thomas Aquinas • passionate opponent of the Templars • defender of centralized royal power and its superiority to religious power • propagator of the codification of French law and need for development of the school system • critic of legal and tax systems •

Du Bois' plan, taken as the first project of Europeanism, was, after its inception, forgotten for five long centuries and then, from the 17th century, buried in the archives of Christine, the Queen of Sweden, and after that in the Vatican, where it was found and brought to light by a French historian and religious thinker, E. Renan. It lacks consistency and is burdened with a lot of diversions without any connection with the main idea. He appealed for the creation of a union of European Christian countries. Peace among them should be ensured by criminal laws against war and by a supranational law court. He did not think about a universal monarchy in Europe (even though he very often preferred the hegemonistic interests of his master, Philip the Comely, and he denounced the power of the Pope). A united Christian Europe should be a federation governed by a Council in which the monarchs would lose nothing of their independence. He suggested the expulsion of all who intruded on friendly relations in Europe to the Orient, where they should discharge their militaristic leanings in the fight against "the infidel". As an extreme measure against enemies of peace, he recommended that their territories should be encircled and trade with them blocked, which, in his opinion, seemed to have a stronger and more reliable effect than weapons. Du Bois' principle of the absolute state and the reigning monarch's sovereignty was also the main weak point of his project for the unification of Europe, because the integrating elements in it appear to be practically ineffective against this principle.

Pierre Du Bois. In: E. Renan, Histoire littéraire de la France. Paris 1873.
De recuperatione Terre Sancte. Paris 1891.

ELIOT THOMAS STEARNS

* 1888 St. Louis   † 1965 London

"I have just emphasized that no European culture can exist if individual countries are isolated from one another. Now I can add that no European culture can exist if the countries are pushed into the very same identity. The unity we need has to contain multiformity. ... Now it is valid for the literature of each nation that it can rejuvenate itself, develop new creative strength, and discover new language possibilities if two presumptions have been fulfilled: firstly, it must be able to accept and process impulses from outside, and secondly it must get back to its own sources and learn from them. ... unity, in contrast with political-organizational unity, does not ask us to recognize one single bond of faithfulness. ... It is wrong to believe that the only duty of an individual is his duty towards the state. What is an absolute exaggeration is to believe that the supreme duty of each individual is his duty towards a super-state."

• British poet, dramatist, and literary critic of American origin • studies of philosophy and literary science at renowned universities - Harvard, the Sorbonne, Oxford • permanent stay in London • short period of teaching • after World War I work for London Lloyd's Bank • Director of the Faber and Faber publishing house • systematic studies of English and world literature • knowledge of all world languages • 1948 the Nobel Prize for Literature •

He was interested above all in Europe as a cultural entity and he also tried to analyse the relationship between politics and culture. Like many others, he emphasized the heritage of Ancient Rome and its ideas, as he found them especially in the works of Virgil, in whose world of values he could see numerous parallels with the values of the world of Christianity. In his "Contributions to the Concept of Culture" he spoke about the spiritual organism of Europe, the extinction of which would mean that the economic and political organization of this continent would no longer involve unifying Europe but only organizing masses of human beings who would be able to speak various languages but would have nothing to say. He took the common cultural richess as a true bond among Europeans, which gives us much more than the best-meant political and economic organization, for, in contrast with this, cultural unity in no way means doing away with, but rather accepting, the variety of unions. Poetry in particular serves him as a proof of how its national likeliness draws on a lot of European elements (he exemplified it on England) and, at the same time, how much it influences the poetry of other nations. In all other spheres of the arts, too, he is able to find three basic components: local traditions, the common European tradition, and the way European countries influence one another. Eliot's considerations are valuable by virtue of being Europeanist ones but at the same time facing Europeanism being over-simplified into technocratic and equalizing dimensions.

Beiträge zum Begriff der Kultur. Frankfurt a. M. 1949.
Selected Essays. London 1961.
Zum Begriff der Kultur. München 1961.
Eseje [Essays]. Bratislava 1972.

ERASMUS DESIDERIUS OF ROTTERDAM

* 1469 (1466) Rotterdam   † 1536 Basel

"But the ultimate in criminal plotting has been reached when the rulers find out that where the nation is unified, their power is unsteady, but where the nation is split, their power is strong; and then they provoke people in a cunning way in order wilfully to foment war and to divide the unity of the nation at the same time and then to exploit it shamelessly in its disaster. ... If only we could expel this pest to the farthest islands! If Christians are limbs of the same body, why do they not enjoy happiness with one another?"

• Dutch theologian and philosopher • greatest humanistic thinker of the Renaissance • in 1486 involuntary admission to the monastery in Steyen • 1492 ordained priest • 1493 allowed to live outside the cloister • 1492 secretary of the bishop of Cambrai • 1495-1499 studies at the Sorbonne in Paris - the beginning of his literary activities • 1498 his first visit to England • friendship with Thomas More • further studies in Paris and Leuven • 1506-1509 stay in Italy • Doctorate in theology in Turin • in Rome - acknowledgement and admiration by educated cardinals and the Pope • 1509-1514 stay in England - doctor's degrees at Oxford and Cambridge Universities • Professor of theology and Greek at Cambridge • 1516 royal counsellor at the court of Charles V in Brabant • 1518-1521 Professor at Leuven • 1521-1529 his life in Basel - the climax of his scientific work and immense publishing activities • departure for Catholic Freiburg after the Reformation reversal in Basel • 1535 return to Basel •

Unlike his contemporary, the anti-European Macchiavelli, who was enthusiastic for unscrupulous sovereign power and the art of war, Erasmus thought that war was sweet only for those who had not become familiar with it and he did not appreciate warriors as people worth admiring. He was so closely connected with Europe and Europeanism by his life and work (if he had a homeland, it was the whole of the Continent) that he is usually referred to as the first conscious European. He used Latin as a supranational language, as an all-European link. He leaned on the tradition of European Christian morals, he believed in the equality of all nations and races, and he laboured for their peaceful co-existence. He pinned certain hopes on Charles V, whose counsellor he was. The idea of Erasmism (as mentioned by Stefan Zweig) connected, and still connects, all the inhabitants of Europe who distinguish themselves by having a shared European feeling. (The European Union acknowledges his heritage, for instance by a major educational project called Erasmus.)

Enchiridion militis christiani. 1503.
Opus de conscribendis epistolis. Paris 1536.
Omnia opera. Basileae 1541.
Against War. Boston 1907.
Důvěrné hovory [Intimate Talks]. Praha 1913.
Klage des Friedens. Leipzig 1934.
Hlasatel humanistických a mírových myšlenek
    [A Herald of Humanistic and Peace Thoughts]. Praha 1958.
Chvála bláznovství [Praise of Madness]. Praha 1969.
Triumf a tragika bláznivosti [The Triumph and Tragedy of Being Mad].
    Bratislava 1985.

FICHTE JOHANN GOTTLIEB

* 1762 Rammenau   † 1814 Berlin

"If war is to be abolished, the reason for wars has to be abolished. Every country has to get what is reasonable for its needs, and what they aim at gaining by means of a war - their natural boundary. From now on they have nothing to demand from another nation, as they have got what they had been looking for."

• representative of German classical philosophy • studies of theology, law, and philosophy at Jena, Leipzig, and Wittenberg Universities • private tutor in Zürich and Königsberg • study of Kant's works • 1792 Professor at Jena University - accusation of atheism - dismissal in 1799 • after the battle near Jena a fighter for liberation from the Napoleonic army • 1808 his famous "Speeches to the German Nation" - appeal for unification of the German nation and for resistance to occupation • 1809 Professor at Berlin • 1811 first Rector of Berlin University • 1813 volunteer in the war against Napoleon •

He might be taken as the first great European theorist of nationalism, a herald of a strangely unnatural conception of the unification of Europe. He respected Rousseau's and Kant's ideas and admired the Great French Revolution, but he strongly objected to Napoleon's efforts to unify Europe by bayonets. In 1796 he drew up a plan for a union of nations in his "A Brief Survey of International and Cosmopolitan Law". He wanted to bring freedom and peace to Europe by putting the nations in straitjackets of autarchy. He considered colonial expansion one of the main causes of the disintegration of Europe and of the rise of greediness for war in it. He recommended the nations to be closed inside their natural borders, within which they ought to be able to satisfy their economic potential as much as possible and thus would not have to long for any expansion. He considered the division of the Europe of that day as a historical inevitability and he advocated the general introduction of "a closed business state" (he elaborated this idea in his work of the same title). He suggested the closing of borders, a ban on the exchange of goods, the introduction of different currencies, etc. In the end even international cultural exchanges and travelling should be cut out (with the exception of scientists and "top" artists). The state that would be at the pinnacle of culture (for him it was Prussia), would slowly and gradually become the genuine homeland of all the Christians in Europe and it would force (in extremes even by war) its culture on other nations. Science should be an important element unifying mankind. In his works nationalism inevitably leads to totalitarianism. According to his bizarre dialectics, science and culture would, in the long run, unify all of Europe (and the whole world) consisting of "closed secluded business states", into "the only national republic of culture".

Pojem vzdělance [Notion of an Educated Person]. Praha 1971.
Reden an die deutsche Nation. Hamburg 1978.
Der geschlossene Handelstaat. Hamburg 1979.
Výber z diela [Selected Works]. Bratislava 1981.
Schriften zur französischen Revolution. Köln 1989.
Addresses to the German Nation. London 1990.
Grundlage des Naturrechts nach Prinzipen der Wissenschaftslehre.
    Hamburg 1991.
Die Bestimmung des Menschen. Stuttgart 1997.
Werke. Frankfurt a. M. 1997.
Johann Gottlieb Fichte Sämmtliche Werke und Nachlass. Berlin 2001.

FRANTZ CONSTANTIN

* 1817 Börnecke   † 1891 Blasewitz

"It is obvious that such a fe-deration cannot come into exi-stence at the drop of a hat. First it needs a real basis in which it could be rooted and only then could an impulse come out of it... It was Germa-ny, where the splitting of the church came from, which later contributed most to the fall of the western commonwealth of nations, and therefore Germa-ny, first of all, is obliged to stand up for its re-establishment and in this way to regulate the spread of the whole European system towards the better. It would certainly mean some-thing other than the events of 1866, which originated only from the ideas of a great power system and involved us more and more in that old system."

• German politician • studies of mathematics and philosophy • early enthusiasm for political science and practical politics • study journeys round France, Poland, and Hungary • till 1856 employee of the Minis-try of Foreign Affairs • 1856 departure from public service for retirement and for scientific work •

He belongs among the authors whose European prescriptions origi-nated in the experience of the nations to which they belonged, in this case Germany. Frantz expressed his conception first of all in his publi-cation of 1879 called "Federalism". He belonged among the pioneers of German unification and, even though he condemned nationalism, he was able to recognize "the European mission of Germany". In the German nation he could see (in Schelling's words) "a nation of nations", and that is why he (quite uncritically) found a model for Europe in the German union. According to him, the national element had found its aim in the fight with absolutism and therefore it had to recede into the background. A union of Central and Northern European countries should become the core of a unified Europe. This bloc would, with the help of England, keep a firm grip on France and Russia - countries which should only join the union in the future in a more positive political atmosphere. His considerations reached beyond the European framework as they took into account even the incorporation of the USA, in which case a global Christian union would arise. He rejected the role of the superpowers, which he said had done much less for freedom, progress, and culture than the small states, saying that for the future they represented the negation of higher historic, moral, and civilized principles and that was why they had to disappear. This means that he did not see the future for Europe as lying in a system of unstable power alliances of limited duration, but unambiguously in a European federation of states connected by long-term relations.

Die Naturlehre des Staates als Grundlage aller Staatswissenschaft. Leipzig 1870.
Der Nationalliberalismus und Judenherrschaft. München 1874.
Die Genesis der Bismarckschen Aera und ihr Ziel. München 1874.
Der Föderalismus. Mainz 1879.
Die Weltpolitik. Chemnitz 1883.

GASPERI ALCIDE DE

* 1884 Pieve Tesino   † 1954 Sella di Valsugana

"Forget all the dreams about Charlemagne and the Middle Ages! We are talking here about a coalition of democracies, based on the principle of freedom…. We urgently require the foundation of a European federation of free democratic countries, which categorically rejects the principle of absolute state sovereignty, defends the rejection of all purely territorial claims, and favours the creation of a legal community of states with all the institutions and resources necessary for the establishment of a government of collectively organized safety. … Economic co-operation is unavoidably a compromise between the naturally independent requirements of each participating party and superior political interests."

• Italian politician • 1900-1905 studies in Vienna • 1911-1918 deputy of the Imperial Council of Austro-Hungary • publisher of the journal "Il Trentino" • after WWI co-organizer of the Italian Catholic People's Party • from 1921 member of the Italian Parliament for this party • initial advocate of cooperation with Mussolini, later consistently in opposition • 1926 removal from his post as MP for his anti-fascist activities and imprisonment for 16 months • from 1929 withdrawal to seclusion in Vatican library • co-founder of the Italian Christian Democratic Party (PDC) and its leader during the period from 1943 to 1953, until his withdrawal from political life • 1944 Minister of Foreign Affairs • 1945-1953 Prime Minister, and simultaneously 1951-1953 Minister of Foreign

Affairs • 1947 crucial contribution to the elimination of communists and socialists from the government •

Under his leadership, Italy took its most important steps toward integration into a united and democratic Europe. As Prime Minister he signed a peace treaty with the Allies, brought Italy into NATO, and was a co-founder of the European Coal and Steel Community. He became a convinced European, who believed in the establishment of a united Europe. He did all that he could to achieve this aim. He participated in the European Congress in the Hague (1948), where he was elected to the executive committee of the European movement. He supported the creation of the Council of Europe and the European Defence Community, and he continuously explained to the general public why this European policy was necessary. His government was among the first to react positively to the European initiatives of the French government concerning European economic integration. De Gasperi's pro-European spirit profoundly influenced the Italian perception of European issues in the sense of Euro-optimism. For his pro-European activities and the integration of Italy in a unifying Europe, de Gasperi was awarded (the first Italian to do so) the Charlemagne Prize in Aachen in 1952.

De Gasperi e l'Europa degli anni Trenta. Roma 1974.
Discorsi politici. Roma 1976.
Scritti politici di Alcide de Gasperi. Milano 1979.
Scritti di politica internazionale, 1933-1938. Città del Vaticano 1981.
Alcide De Gasperi e la politica internazio. Roma 1990.
Alcide de Gasperi in Parlamento, 1921-1954. Roma 1990.
Quale politica per quale famiglia in Europa. Milano 1991.

GENTZ FRIEDRICH VON

* 1764 Wroclaw   † 1832 Vienna

"The natural federative composition of Europe should be organized so skilfully that in a big political mass every balance should be counter-balanced somewhere."

• German politician and journalist • studies of law and philosophy at Königsberg University • from 1785 in Prussian civil service • 1802 imperial council in Vienna • journalistic activity against Napoleon • 1812 confidant and collaborator of Metternich • leader of the protocol at the Vienna Congress and at congresses in Aachen, Carlsbad, Ljubljana, Opava, and Verona • defender of the legitimacy of monarchist power, opponent of liberalism •

A disciple of Kant and, like him, he was at first enthusiastic about the Great French Revolution, but later, under the influence of Edmund Burke's works, one of the most passionate opponents of Jacobinism. His opinions on European problems were very variable. As a European he could see even Tsar Alexander as "a Knight or a General Secretary of Europe", but later he became a completely uncritical defender of the selfish and reactionary policy of Austria and the word Europe turned into an abomination for him. He was also an adherent of the idea that wars were inevitable. In the year 1800 he published a book called "On Ever-Lasting Peace". In it Gentz stated that until that time there had always been suggested three ways leading to ever-lasting peace - a world state, nations closing themselves against one another (Fichte), and a union of states (preserved by the Constitution or a court of arbitration). In the beginning he inclined towards a federative solution of the problem, but later on he adopted a pessimistically critical attitude. In the end he arrived at the opinion that above all Europe needed a balance of power - the Holy Alliance.

On the State of Europe before and after the French Revolution. London 1804.
The Dangers and Advantages of the Present State of Europe. London 1806.
Über den ewigen Frieden. Manheim 1838.
Friedrich von Gentz Staatsschriften und Briefe. München 1921.
The French and American Revolutions Compared. Houston 1975.
Fragments upon the Balance of Power in Europe. London 1979.
Fragmente aus der neusten Geschichte des politischen Gleichgewichts in Europa. Hildesheim 1997.
Gesammelte Schriften. Hildesheim 1997.
Vom dem politischen Zustande von Europa vor und nach der Französischen Revolution. Hildesheim 1997.

GIOBERTI VINCENZO

* 1801 Turin   † 1852 Paris

"Europe is, from a legal point of view, what Italy represents to a limited extent, which means the cumulation of a lot of states which need a mutual relationship (without losing their individuality) and have the necessary preconditions for it, but at the same time are separated and in a hostile mood because of their mutual disbelief and hostility."

• Italian philosopher, politician, journalist • studies of theology and philosophy • 1831 chaplain at the court of the Sardinian King • arrest for suspicion of contacts with "Young Italy" • 1833 expulsion - departure for France, later for Belgium • 1847 return to Italy • Professor at Turin University • political activity • 1848 at the head of the Sardinian government • 1849 ambassador in France • 1850 emigration to France •

His view of European unity often had an Italian timbre. He became involved in unifying Italy, which he labelled "The Orient of the West", and attributed to it the role of the leading European nation. The Pope should be the patron and creator of a European union, with Rome as its centre. He proclaimed a theory of dialectic transition from a city state to a nation, from a nation to Europe, and from Europe to the world. He saw the Greeks as the forefathers of European ideas. He also took Europe to be the most important continent, and explained this fact by its location, the climate, natural conditions, religion, and the quality of the race. Christianity, in his opinion, was progressing by leaps and bounds towards a peaceful control of not only Europe but the whole world.

GIOBERTI VINCENZO

Prolegomini al Primato. Torino 1848.
Der moderne Jesuitismus. Leipzig 1849.
Die geheimen Pläne der Jesuiten der Neuzeit. Eger 1909.
Gioberti. Milano 1952.
Del rinnovamento civile d'Italia. Roma 1969.
Scritti scelti. Torino 1970.

GOETHE JOHANN WOLFGANG VON

* 1749 Frankfurt am Main   † 1832 Weimar

"It is a strange thing indeed - hatred among nations. You will always find it in the strongest and most violent savage at the lowest levels of culture. But there is a level at which it practically disappears, and that is where we somehow get above nations in a way and feel both the happiness and sorrow of a neighbouring nation as if it were our own nation."

• German poet, prose writer, and thinker • wide range of interests - painting, theory of arts, natural sciences • 1765-1768 studies of law at Leipzig University • 1768-1770 stay in Frankfurt am Main - his first collection of poems • 1770-1771 Strasbourg University • meeting with Herder, their friendship • Doctorate in Law • legal probationer in Wetzlar • from 1775 permanent stay in Weimar • prominent state offices at the court of Grand Duke Karl Augustus • 1786 first journey to Italy - influenced by classical culture • devotee of the ideals of humanism and harmony of man • 1794 beginning of friendship and cooperation with F. Schiller (the "Sturm und Drang" Movement) • 1794-1805 most fruitful literary period: ballads, novels • 1825-1831 accomplishment of his novel writing and the climax of his writing poetry •

We can find very few specifically European statements in his works, but Europe is present in nearly everything he said or wrote. He was not very interested in plans for political unification. Goethe rejected nationalism - both German and French, as well as that of Europe; he appreciated European virtues on the one hand but also admired the American lifestyle, for example, and supposed that America was taking over not only the cultural heritage of Europe but also its epoch-making role. He believed that technology would push Europe to greater and greater unification. Big projects (he praises them at the end of "Faust" too) were, for him, a harbinger of the coming unity. Intellectually, he was very close to Staël. He could see the real unity of Europe in culture and he particularly emphasized the importance of literature, in which it is necessary to move away from the national to the European and the global. He urged well-educated and better people to operate in a conciliatory way in the relationships among nations and he wished that the free exchange of ideas and feelings would intensify the wealth and general well-being of mankind. He affirmed that an international community needed moral laws which could help nations integrate into one harmonious unit.

Vilém Meister Praha 1920.
Gespräche zu Riemer. Zürich 1948-1954.
Faust. Praha 1982.
Selected Works. New York 2000.
Tagebücher. Stuttgart 2000.

GORBACHEV MIKHAIL SERGEYEVICH

* 1931 Privolno

"We had a large European house before our eyes: there were different rooms, but communication among them was possible; and it would be the only house whose inhabitants would respect common rules."

• Soviet and Russian politician • studies of law at the Lomonosov University in Moscow • from 1952 member of the Communist Party of the USSR and an official in regional organizations of the Communist Party • from 1971 member of the Central Committee of the Communist Party • from 1980 member of the Politburo of the Central Committee of the Communist Party • 1985-1991 Secretary-General of the Communist Party • 1988-1990 chairman of the Praesidium of the Supreme Soviet • 1989-1991 the first and last President of the USSR • 1990 Nobel Peace Prize • 1991 political fall following the disintegration of the USSR • 1996 unsuccessful presidential candidate in Russia •

Although Mikhail Gorbachev was a communist politician, he nevertheless belongs among those personalities of the twentieth century who took part in creating a new, integrated Europe. He recognised the depth of the crisis in Soviet society and the economy, and he tried to resolve it in the spirit of reform communism, but, at the same time, to maintain the power of the Communist Party. These reforms are known as "perestroika" and "glasnost". Glasnost brought about a significant relaxation of totalitarian conditions, public discussion, journalistic and cultural freedom, and a re-evaluation of Soviet history. In 1989 he introduced a new idea of foreign policy, which he called "building a common European home". This consisted of dissolving the existing military blocs and creating a single all-European security organization based on the principle of collective security. Rather than a geographic or political entity, Gorbachev perceived Europe as a cultural community based on democratic norms, and including not only Europe but also North America. In the interest of an agreement with the West, he abandoned the aggressive Soviet foreign policy (war in Afghanistan) and he strove to limit the nonproductive and armaments programmes, which were debilitating the state. He participated in many summits which were very important for world disarmament and for bringing together the East and the West. In 1987 he signed a treaty with Ronald Reagan in Washington concerning the liquidation of medium-range missiles. In 1991 he signed a Strategic Arms Limitation Treaty with George Bush Sr. in Moscow that dealt with a reduction in the numbers of strategic weapons. His policies provoked a great reaction in the countries of the communist bloc, and by the end of 1989 they actually led to the fall of the communist regimes in the Eastern bloc and, eventually, in the USSR itself. Although perestroika did not go outside the framework of reform communism, it had a significant impact on the commencement of the democratic changes in Eastern Europe and on change in political conditions in Europe.

Gorbachev created the preconditions for Russia, which was weakened but still powerful, to remain in dignified existence, and enabled the European nations which had been subjugated by Russia to decide freely about their future destiny. He enabled all of this to happen in an essentially peaceful and serene way. For his invaluable contribution to world peace and to the democratic transformations in Central and Eastern Europe, Gorbachev received not only the Nobel Peace Prize but also many other prestigious international prizes, the Czech "Order of the White Lion" among them. The consequences of Gorbachev's policies were more far-reaching than he had originally intended, and they opened up the possibility of the integration of the entire European continent.

Perestroika. New Thinking for Our Country and the World. Cambridge, New
York 1987.

Výbor z projevů a statí [Selected Speeches and Essays]. Praha 1988.

Speech before the Parliamentary Assembly of the Council of Europe.
Strasbourg 1989.

Address at the Meeting of the Leaders of States Participating in the Conference
on Security and Cooperation in Europe. Moscow 1990.

Evropeiskie tetradi. Moskva 1994.

Reformátoři nebývají šťastni [Reformers are not Usually Happy]. Praha 1995.

Memoirs. New York 1996.

The New World Order. Abu Dhabi 1998.

GÖRRES JOHANN JOSEPH VON

* 1776 Koblenz   † 1848 Munich

"Let Germany become the honorary head of the European Republic, a negotiating power in all disputes because of its status, location, convictions; everything in it drives towards peace, nothing towards conquest: it is a great separating and protecting power, keeping apart the Orient and the Occident, the north and the south, a great point of support of the European state system, a natural centre of the new, the larger Holy Roman Empire which would be established as a union of nations by the Christian alliance under quite new liberal conditions."

• German historian, philosopher, and journalist • adherent of the ideas of the Great French Revolution • disappointment with Napoleon, resignation from politics • from 1804 teacher of physics in Koblenz • 1806-1808 private senior lecturer at Heidelberg University • participant in anti-Napoleon wars of liberation • 1814-1816 publisher of the "Rheinische Merkur" - banned for its advocacy of a unified German constitution • 1819 persecution for publishing the work "Deutschland und Revolution" • emigration • from 1827 Professor of history at Munich University • outstanding representative of the circle of Catholic scientists •

It was he who, among the Romanticists, wrote most about Europe in a contradictory and eccentric way. At first he was thrilled by the Great French Revolution, which "liberated Europe from its monarchs", and suggested establishing an international organization under the leadership of the French Republic, but after Napoleon's coup d'état he switched over to the position of the Restoration and later the Holy Alliance. In his article on "The European Republic" and in his book "The Holy Alliance and the Nations at the Congress in Verona" he proclaimed the Germans as the standard-bearers of the merits of Europe and welcomed the Holy Alliance as the beginning of the European Republic. He became a herald of the historic mission of Germany which, "if it finds a new Wallenstein", would bring under its control the whole Continent up to the border with Asia. In his work "Europe and Revolution" he attacked the Reformation as the second original sin because he said it had destroyed, together with other disasters (e.g. Islam, revolution, and Napoleon), "Europe - my fortress". He often only repeated the ideas of de Maistre, just dressed in German clothing. He considered dangerous for his vision of Germanic-Catholic Europe not Russia - "a colony of Europe", which would join it voluntarily - but Asia and America.

Glauben und Wissen. München 1805.
Gesammelte Schriften. München 1854-1860.
Ausgewählte Schriften. München 1921.
Geist und Geschichte. Einsiedeln 1957.

HABSBURG OTTO VON

* 1912 Reichenau

"Allow me to emphasize once more: we are facing especially the task of the re-unification of Europe. ... Central Europe is playing a special role here..., since the Pan-European idea rose on the ground of the old Danubian monarchy, in Bohemia. At the moment, all Europe is to be restored from its geographic, historic, and spiritual centre. ... Europe has to regain its Slavonic dimension, but at the same time the European dimension, which has been oppressed for dozens of years, has to be awakened to a new life among the Slavs. ...

The Czech lands - I mean also Moravia and Austrian Silesia - have the right of the first-born baby in Europe. They can put stress on it if they are going to be restored in the spirit of Christianity. In this spirit national hatred and deflection from religion, too, which still exist in Bohemia, could be overcome. ... If we do not find the way back to faith, Europe is not going to survive."

• German politician of Austrian origin • son of the last Austro-Hungarian Emperor Karl I • childhood in Switzerland and Spain • from 1930 studies of law at Leuven University • 1937 Doctorate in Social and Juristic Sciences • 1938 author of the protest against the Anschluss of Austria • accusation of high treason and persecution by the Nazis • departure to France, from 1940 in the USA • organizer of help to Austrian refugees • after the War short stay in Austria • from 1946 in France, from 1954 permanently in Germany • 1947 head of the Pan-European Union • 1950 founder of the European Documentary and Information

Centre in Madrid • 1961 abandonment of dynastic claims • 1979 elected to the European Parliament •

The development of Europe after 1918 did not give him a chance to restore the monarchy, the successor to whose throne he was, even in a form restricted to Hungary or Austria, but his role in European politics has never been negligible. Otto von Habsburg was an opponent of nationalism, especially of its Nazi version, but also of Stalinist totalitarian internationalism. That is why he, as a politician and political scientist, was involved in the democratic unification of European nations. His unifying ideas originated in the principles of the free will of nations and the social market economy. For him, the unity of Europe did not mean only economic and political relations among nations, but, above all, the developing of the European spirit, based on Christianity. His ideas were close to those of the founder of the Pan-European Union, Earl Coudenhove-Kalergi. Together with him, he performed numerous international activities aimed at European integration and contributed to the beginnings of its being realized after World War II. After Coudenhove-Kalergi's death, Otto von Habsburg became President of the Pan-European Union. As a German citizen and Christian Democrat, he was elected to the European Parliament and he worked there as a member of the political committee for Central and Eastern Europe. His historic relationship with the Czech Lands has been reflected in his continuing support of our incorporation into all European structures.

Brennpunkte der Europafrage. 1958.
Entscheidung für Europa. Innsbruck 1958.
Soziale Ordnung von Morgen.Wien 1958.
Europa-Grossmacht oder Schlachtfeld. München 1965.
Beiträge zum Sudetendeutschen Tag. München 1967.
Idee Europa. München 1977.
Geschichte und Zukunft einer übernationalen Ordnung. Wien 1986.
Europa im Umbruch. Flaach 1990.
Return to the Center. Riverside 1993.
Úvahy o Evropě [Reflections on Europe]. Praha 1993.
Friedensmacht Europa. Wien 1995.
Die paneuropäische Idee: eine Vision wird Wirklichkeit. Wien 1999.

HAVEL VÁCLAV

* 1936 Prague

"I can imagine Europe in the twenty-first century as a confederation. I can imagine that some of today's structures will one day change into the organs of such a confederation, ... I can imagine that some of today's European institutions will gradually grow into this confederation and dissolve in it, while others will remain permanent parts of her varied internal structure. Confederated Europe is therefore a very nice, reasonable, desirable, and even probable futurological vision. But not only that: we can imagine even more: that the European consciousness will quickly embrace this vision, take it for its own, and that it will quietly but steadily begin to think and work in its spirit, so that even the most politically diverse individuals, states, and international European organizations or institutions will always respect this vision and take the direction which the vision indicates."

• Czech dramatist and politician • one of the key figures of Czech dissent • 1962-1966 studies of dramaturgy at DAMU (Academy of Dramatic Arts) in Prague • 1961-1968 assistant director and literary manager of the theatre Na zábradlí • his most important plays written in the 1960s • 1968-1969 head of the Club of Independent Writers • 1976 one of the leading protagonists and initiators of "Charta 77" • 1977 and 1978 repeated imprisonment • 1979 4 years and six months' imprisonment, release before the end of the sentence on account of health problems in 1983 • 1989 initiator and co-author of the "Several

Sentences" manifesto • 1989 leader of the Civic Forum during the "Velvet Revolution" • 1989 President of the Czechoslovak Federal Republic • from 1993 President of the Czech Republic •

By all of his activities during the period of totalitarianism, Václav Havel tried to save the Czech cultural and democratic relationship with free Europe. As early as 1975, in an open letter to the Czechoslovak President, he philosophically analysed Czechoslovak society and he warned against its substantial devastation and lagging behind Europe.

After the defeat of communism in 1989, in important political functions (and in cooperation with another pro-European former dissident, Jiří Dienstbier, who later became the Minister of Foreign Affairs), he strove for the quickest and most complete possible integration of the country into European structures. The policy statement of the Civic Forum from 26 November 1989, in the formulation of which Havel had a substantial share, proclaimed the Czechoslovak desire to regain a dignified position in Europe by means of the country's incorporation into European integration.

Havel visualized European integration in the form of a confederation. The futurological dimension of the confederation is represented by his idea that if all global processes move toward integration (or globalization), so much the more this must apply to Europe.

The second dimension of his understanding of European integration is wholly contemporary. According to Havel, it is important to work on the platform of the European Union on the unification and compatibility of some systems, such as energy systems, transportation systems, communication systems etc., while, for the time being, it is not so vitally important to be concerned about problems of security, which rather fall within the competence of NATO. However, it is also very important somehow to incorporate the Council of Europe into this confederation.

Havel has always emphasized the solution of ethical problems and he has therefore considered the need for a European moral codex.

HAVEL VÁCLAV

Moc bezmocných [Power of the Powerless]. Praha 1990.
Dopisy Olze [Letters to Olga]. Brno 1990.
Do různých stran [In Various Directions]. Praha 1990.
Projevy [Speeches]. Praha 1990.
Paříž-Praha. Intelektuálové v Evropě Paris-Prague. Intellectuels en Europe. Praha 1994.
Vážení občané! [Dear citizens!] Praha 1994.
Václav Havel '94. Praha 1995.
Václav Havel '95. Praha 1996.
Václav Havel '96. Praha 1997.
Václav Havel '97. Praha 1998.
Moral in Zeiten der Globalisierung. Reinbek bei Hamburg 1998.
Identikit Europe. London 2001.

HEGEL GEORG WILHELM FRIEDRICH

* 1770 Stuttgart † 1831 Berlin

"The history of the world advances from the east to the west, therefore Europe is the end of world history, Asia its beginning...; although the Earth makes a sphere, history does not make a circle, it has a certain beginning, and that is Asia. Here the outer Sun - the material one - rises, and it sets in the west; but here in the west the inner Sun of self-confidence rises and spreads a stronger glow."

• leading representative of German classical philosophy • 1788-1793 studies of theology and philosophy at Tübingen University - a schoolmate of F. Schelling • affection for the Great French Revolution • 1793-1801 private tutor in Bern and Frankfurt am Main • further studies of history, economics, law, and natural sciences • 1801-1807 private senior lecturer and later Professor of philosophy at Jena University • 1816 called to Heidelberg University • 1818-1831 Professor at Berlin University • 1829 Rector of same •

European issues can be seen in his works only as a part of general philosophical considerations and theories about an idea, the realization of which (the materialization of the spirit) is reflected in the history of the world. In his "Lectures on the Philosophy of History" he described the development of Asia, the ancient world, and new Europe as if it were only spiritual development, which had found its historical purpose and final destination in Europe and Europe alone, that was at issue. When searching for the historic missions of individual European nations, he came to the supra-evaluation of the Germans and Germany as a spokesman of "the spirit of the new world". This was then made use of by his right-wing adherents as being able to underline the role of the Prussian state. (A contemporary of his, the French philosopher Théodore Jouffroy, agreed with his evaluation of Europe but attributed the leading position to the French.) He did not attach any great importance to the Slavonic nations, as "non-historic ones". His theory of war as an inevitable historic feature was also a matter in dispute.

Vorlesungen über die Philosophie der Geschichte. Leipzig 1928.
Filosofie, umění a náboženství a jejich vztah k mravnosti a státu [Philosophy, Arts, and Religion and Their Relation to Morality and a State]. Praha 1943.
Filozofia dejín [Philosophy of History]. Bratislava 1957.
Fenomenologie ducha [Phenomenology of the Spirit]. Praha l960.
Die Vernunft in der Geschichte. Berlin 1966.
Recht. Staat. Geschichte. Stuttgart 1981.
Základy filosofie práva [Foundations of Philosophy of Law]. Praha 1992.
Philosophy of Right. Amherst 1996.
Lectures on the History of Philosophy. Bristol 1999.
Philosophie des Rechts. New York 1999.
Political Writings. New York 1999.

HEINE HEINRICH

* 1797 Düsseldorf † 1856 Paris

"Virgin Europe is engaged to the handsome genius of liberty; they are embracing each other, being brought into ecstasy by their first kiss."

• German poet, prose writer, and journalist • from 1819 studies of law in Bonn, Göttingen, and Berlin • interest in literature and history • attendance of Hegel's lectures in Berlin • permanent guest at literary salons • 1825 Doctorate in Law • conversion from Judaism to Protestantism • literary activity - lyrical poems, essays on travels, sketches • critic of nationalism and militarism • 1831 leaving for Paris - friendship with H. Balzac, G. Sand, A. Dumas • rich publishing activities • tendencies to bring the French and the Germans together • 1835 his works prohibited in Germany • 1845 onset of a serious illness - life in seclusion - nevertheless interested in the fates of Germany and Europe •

Like Goethe, he never dealt with European thoughts systematically, but, in spite of that, Europe is omnipresent in his works. In the beginning he agreed with Herder's and Fichte's idea of a Europe of nationalities as a necessary stage of historic development. His ideas of a union of nations were federative ones, but in them we can find unexpected sways from liberal universalism up to Germanic nationalism. In the preface to his work "Germany - a Winter Tale", which was written in the period of the awakening of great hopes for the freedom of Europe, he wrote that literally the whole Continent, or even the whole world, would be German. Heine understood the idea of a nation in the sense of Mazzini's "the

Internationale of the Nationalists" and he wanted to preserve local liberties and diversity against "the terrible equalizers of Europe" (represented for him by the likes of Richelieu, Robespierre, or the financier Rothschild). Heine repeatedly warned against the fatality of German - French conflicts for Europe and he was also terrified by the vision expressed by Napoleon on St. Helena, i. e. that Europe could soon become a Russian monarchy.

Henri Heine ses vues sur l'Allemagne et les révolutions européennes. Paris 1939.
O Německu [On Germany]. Praha 1951.
Z cest [Travels]. Praha 1952.
Dopisy [Letters]. Praha 1967.
Písně lásky a hněvu [Songs of Love and Anger]. Praha 1980.
Deutschland a Winter's Tale. London 1986.
Memorabilia. 1995.
Unterwegs in Europa. Berlin 1995.
De l'Allemagne. Paris 1998.
Deutschland ein Wintermärchen. Frankfurt a. M. 1998.
Ich hab im Traum geweinet. Frankfurt a. M. 1998.
Werke. Berlin 1998.

HERDER JOHANN GOTTFRIED VON

*1744 Mohrungen   † 1803 Weimar

"Providence once gave Europeans scales and measures. Let them measure, let them weigh. However, if they use the wrong measures for their own benefit only, what will happen with the decisive scale of fate in their hands that was commended to them to support the happiness of nations?"

• German philosopher, poet, and theoretician of the "Sturm und Drang" literary movement • 1762-1764 studies of theology, philosophy, and medicine at Königsberg University • student of I. Kant • 1764-1769 teacher and preacher in Riga - first literary and aesthetic works • 1769 studies of the French language and literature in Nantes • encounters with the works of Ch. Montesquieu and J. J. Rousseau • travel to Germany - meeting with G. Lessing and J. W. Goethe • 1771-1776 consistorial counsel in Bückenburg • 1776 called by the monarch to Weimar, at Goethe's intervention • court preacher, later the supreme consistorial counsel •

From Herder's thoughts on the origin and decay of cultures, his ideas on the role of Europe in world history in particular raised ongoing disputes. In our continent, he found the acme of general progress, but he also warned against the revenge of other continents for European colonization and looting. Europe should not isolate itself from other nations, and it should be aware of the general dimension of humanity. As a forerunner of romantic nationalism, he attempted to define "the spirit of a nation". Although he spoke (as a supporter of a theory of geographical races) about Nordic virtues, he also rejected the national superiority of one race over another. He envisaged Europe as a large harp whose universal harmony consisted of the various sounds of all its strings - its nations. His ideas on the historical mission of the Slavonic nations were enthusiastically accepted in the Slavonic part of Europe, as they differed remarkably from what were then the usual unfriendly or contemptuous German approaches. Herder was an advocate of a balance of power in Europe and he dreamed of establishing a European "Republic of Scholars".

Vývoj lidskosti [Development of Humanity]. Praha 1941.
Sämmtliche Werke. Hildesheim 1994.
Vom Geist des Christentums. Weimar 1994.
Ideen zur Philosophie der Geschichte der Menschheit. Bodenhaim 1995.
On World History. Armonk 1996.
Adrastea. Frankfurt a. M. 2000.

Hofmannsthal Hugo von

* 1874 Vienna   † 1929 Rodaun

"Great people take their own nations for their destinies, Europe for an experience..., Europe is where a great idea is thought. Where the idea appears in the national sphere, it is waiting for its flow into the universal. Nowadays, as in the days of Anaximandros, any philosophy is European. Every noble political idea which lives on is European. Every fruitful piece of knowledge of the past is European. Every profound observation of non-Europe is European. (And what do we need more than a profound, brand-new, entirely clear view of non-Europe?)"

• Austrian poet, prose writer, playwright, and essayist • studies of law and Romance studies at Vienna University • influence of French symbolism • initiator of the "Salzburg Festival" • author of dramas in verse • librettist of R. Strauss • collector and publisher of old German literary works (1915-1917 "Austrian Library", 1922-1923 "German Reader") •

When, at his friend C. J. Burckhardt's urging, Hofmannstahl, the poet, started his prosaic work "Europe" contemplating the meaning of the word Europe and whether it still (or again) made sense for a person to feel like a European or if it was only a memory of the atmosphere of the past - the ancient world, humanism - he came to the conclusion that, as with many other great concepts, it was also possible to cast doubt on "Europe" and "European", but they should by no means be jettisoned because the further spiritual life of this continent depended on the defence and rehabilitation of these concepts. Like many others, he saw a deadly danger in nationalism, which might be overpowered not by being radically crushed but by applying the power of Europe's spiritual heritage, as well as the spiritual present. The concept of "Europe" cannot be given a new content and life by sentimental evocation of the past, or by taking something away from and adding something new to the "national principle". The only way is that our souls will be elevated by the power of experiencing the highest achievements of each nation. Though Europe in his day seemed to him to be weak and afflicted by unmitigated disintegration, beyond the prophets of doom and chaos, beyond the chauvinists and cosmopolitans, he saw outstanding personalities - "Europeans" who gave the continent a chance of creative restoration and who would make the concept of Europe great again.

Gesamelte Werke in drei Bänden. Berlin 1934.
Europa. Frankfurt a. M. 1955.
Gedichte. Stuttgart 2000.

HUGO VICTOR MARIE

* 1802 Besançon   † 1885 Paris

"Welcome Europe! Let her enter her home, let her take Paris, a city that belongs to her and to which she belongs. ... In a granite block put in the middle of the old monarchic domain, the French nation cut the space for the first layer of masonry of a building of the future that will one day be called the United Nations of Europe. ... Thus we will have Europe as a republic. ... We will see how the spirit of conquest turns into a spirit of discovery; we will have a generous brotherhood of nations instead of a wild brotherhood of emperors; we will have a homeland without  *borders, a budget without spongers, trade without customs tariffs, communication without bounds, education without brutality, young people without the barracks, courage without fighting, justice without a scaffold, life without murder, the forest without a tiger, a ploughshare without a sword, words without declamations, conscience without a yoke, truth without dogma, God without a priest, heaven without hell, love without hate. ... Europe, you are the only folk and you want the only thing: Peace!"*

• French poet, playwright, prose writer, and essayist • leading representative of French Romanticism • first award of the French Academy for a book of poetry at the age of fifteen • launch of career as a professional writer in 1822 - simultaneous entry into politics • 1830 official poet of the July monarchy • 1830-1843 extensive writing of poems, plays, and novels • 1841 nominated a member of the French Academy

• 1843-1848 intellectual and political development from liberal monarchism to democratism • 1848 convinced Republican - elected deputy to the Constituent and Legislative Assembly • 1851 after the fall of the Republic, an uncompromising opponent of Napoleon III, leaving France for exile (Brussels, Jersey, and Guernsey) • refusal of amnesty • 1852-1870 rich literary output: collections of lyrics and political satire, philosophical poems, culmination of his novel writing • 1870 return to France • 1871 elected deputy to the National Assembly • 1876 National Assembly senator • defender of liberal democracy until his death in 1885 • on the day of his death, a day of national mourning in France • burial in the Pantheon in Paris •

A great lyric poet of the idea of Europeanism; besides Cattane, he is said to have been the first user of the term "The United States of Europe" (in 1851, in his address to the French Parliament). In his frequent messages, he often used the term "my European fellow-countrymen". Shocked by the Turkish massacres in Serbia, he called for all-European responsibility for anything that happened anywhere in Europe and in this context, he especially emphasized the necessity of European unification. Unlike many other French thinkers, he was not a French nationalist, though some of his statements - read out of context - might be interpreted in this way. As a matter of fact he mistook France for Europe and Europe for France. He was proud of the French contributions to European progress, but he did not ask for any reciprocal privileges or the right to dictate to other countries. He did not long for a bigger France ruling over Europe but he dreamed of the French nation's contribution of its best to the uniting of all European nations. Under a flag of humanity, France was to merge with Europe. On 21st August 1848, he solemnly declared this hope as the President of the Congress on Peace Issues in Paris, and he exerted all his extraordinary authority both as a writer and man for the realization of his dream.

HUGO VICTOR MARIE

The Prospects of Republicanism. London 1854.
Taten und Worte. Stuttgart 1876-1877.
Actes et Paroles Pour la Serbie. Paris 1882.
Francii a světu [To France and the World]. Praha 1953.
Beru si slovo [Taking Permission to Speak]. Praha 1985.
Les poètes et l'Europe. Paris 1993.
Correspondance 1833-1883. Paris 2001.
Ecrits politiques. Paris 2001.

HUSSERL EDMUND

* 1859 Prostějov   † 1938 Freiburg

"The necessary condition for this understanding is that the phenomenon of 'Europe' is grasped in its heart. To understand the nuisance of the present 'crisis', the phenomenon of Europe would have had to be drawn up as a historical teleology of infinite rational objectives; it would have had to be shown how the European 'world' was born from rational ideas, i. e. from the spirit of philosophy. 'A crisis' then might seem obvious as an apparent failure of rationalism. The reason for the failure of rational culture is not, as it has been said, in the spirit of rationalism itself, but only in its alienation... The crisis of European existence has only two solutions: a decay of Europe in alienation of its own rational sense of life, a fall into hostility of spirit and barbarism, or a renaissance of Europe and the spirit of philosophy using the heroism of reason that will overpower naturalism for good and all."

• German philosopher, founder of phenomenology • influence of F. Brentan, B. Bolzano, and G. W. Leibniz • 1901-1915 Professor in Göttingen • 1916-1928 Professor of philosophy at Halle, Göttingen, and Freiburg Universities • critic of skepticism and relativism in philosophy •

In his book "A Crisis of European Sciences and Transcendental Phenomenology", he dealt, among other things, with then oft-discussed European issues such as liberty, European crises, and the will to fight destiny. His answer to the question about the spiritual shape of Europe was the ancient world, whose creators were, in Husserl's view, the ancient Greeks. Greek philosophy was the basis of spiritual Europe. Although he did not deny the Babylonian, Egyptian, Chinese, and other legacies of the past, in the Greek nation he found a higher - universal and theoretical - contribution. In this resource, he also saw the way to an analysis and understanding of, and a way out of, the "crisis of European being". Against the philosophical background of European history he did not see this crisis as a dark and impenetrable destiny, but as something quite understandable and transparent. He considered weariness to be the biggest threat to Europe, and encouraged all "good Europeans" to fight courageously against the deadly blaze of apathy and the fire of despair over the human mission of the West. He appealed to them to raise the Phoenix of a new meaning of life from the ashes and to cultivate spirituality as a prerequisite for a bright future for mankind.

Krize evropských věd a transcendentální fenomenologie [A Crisis of European Sciences and Transcendental Phenomenology]. Praha 1972.
Die Krisis der europäischen Wissenschaften und die transzendentale Phänomenologie. Dordrecht 1991.
Gesammelte Schriften. Hamburg 1992.
La crise de l'humanité européenne et la philosophie. Paris 1994.
Die Krisis des europäischen Menschentums und die Philosophie. Weinheim 1995.
A Key to Husserl's Ideas. Milwaukee 1996.
Collected Works. Kluwer 2001.
Natur und Geist. Dordrecht 2001.

JASPERS KARL

* 1883 Oldenburg   † 1969 Basel

"The freedom of a European searches for extremes, for depth of inner conflicts. A European comes through despair to a new-born confidence, through nihilism to constituting the sense of being ... . Europe created an anti-position to each position. ... Therefore, it is willing to take issues coming from outside not only as a contradiction but to recreate them into an element of its own being. Europe knows monumental orders and the unrest of revolutions. It is conservative and realizes the most radical breakthroughs. It knows the reconciliation of religious devoutness and outbreaks of nihilistic negation. It celebrates Christian-universal ideas of authority as well as the idea of Enlightenment. It builds large systems in philosophy and lets them be broken down again by prophets announcing truths. It lives in the consciousness of a large public complex as well as in personal and private intimacy."

• German philosopher and physician leading figure of Existentialism • initially studies of law, later medicine - specialization in psychiatry • from 1908 assistant at the Psychiatric Clinic in Heidelberg • 1913 inclination to philosophy • 1913 senior lecturer, 1921 Professor of philosophy at Heidelberg University • after Hitler's assumption of power in 1933, expulsion from the University • 1937 his professorship cancelled • 1938 forbidden to publish or make public speeches • 1939-1945 scientific work outside the mainstream • publication, immediately after the defeat of fascism, of a philosophical work, "The Question of Guilt" (subtitled "A Contribution to the German Issue") • from 1948 Professor at Basel University •

In his book "Die geistige Situation der Zeit" (1931 - translated as "Man in the Modern Age", 1933), he considered it necessary, before acceding to a fatal catastrophic vision of Europe, to look calmly at the actual position and historical role of Europe and mankind within the Earth's evolution. With such an approach, he found a lot of possibilities for further development - from the death of our culture to the coming of a promising new era. He defined the concept of Europe in three words: liberty, history, and science. In his essay "On the European Spirit" of 1946, he argued that the European understanding of liberty was based on polarities, on the tension between opposites, on historical consciousness, and on the desire for knowledge and understanding.

Die geistige Situation der Zeit. Berlin 1947.
Vom europäischen Geist. München 1947.
Úvod do filozofie [An Introduction to Philosophy]. Praha 1991.

JIŘÍ Z PODĚBRAD (GEORGE OF PODĚBRADY)

* 1420 Poděbrady   † 1471 Prague

"And therefore, as we desire that these wars, pillage, mayhem, fires, and murders that - alas - as we state with pain, have seized Christianity itself from nearly all sides, which plunder fields, devastate towns, ravage countries, and by countless torments destroy kingdoms and principalities, cease and are extirpated, and in praiseful unity, everything is set in a needful state of mutual love and brotherhood, we have decided - according to our best knowledge, after thorough discretion, appealing to the blessing of the Holy Spirit and after the advice and consent of our prelates, princes, grandees, noblemen, and doctors of divine and human law - to establish such an alliance joined in peace, brotherhood, and concord which would, due to its respect for God and preserving the faith, last unshakably and perpetually for us, our heirs and our future successors in the form described below."

• Czech king, able diplomat and politician of the Kunštát family • gained substantial property and significant political influence during the Hussite Wars • 1434 at the Battle of Lipany, fought at the side of the "Peers' Unity" • from 1444 at the head of the Eastern Bohemian 'landfrieds' • 1448 conquest of Prague and inauguration of the Calixtine archbishop Jan Rokycana • main aim - re-establishment of political unity in the country • by artful diplomacy compromise reached between the Calixtines and the Catholic "Strakonice Unity" • 1452 land administrator • 1458 elected the Czech King • new conflict with Rome in 1462 after abolition of the Basel Compactata • attempt to oppose imminent isolation by diplomatic measures • 1462-1464 diplomatic mission to West European sovereigns with a plan for a peace union • 1465 domestic opposition to the King, supported by the Pope • successful fight against the Pope's crusade from 1466 up to his sudden death •

Together with A. Marini, he compiled the first really sophisticated and concrete plan of a solution to Europe's problems. His "Agreement on Peacemaking in All the Christian World" (still somewhat underestimated and sometimes groundlessly labelled as indebted to Pierre Du Bois) was, in five hundred years of European effort, the only project submitted by the head of a state, not by a utopian dreamer, scholar, or an ordinary politician. It was a realistic proposal by a man who, though he disposed of power, did not represent for Europe a danger of the dynastic abuse of the unifying idea. George of Poděbrady was not another aggressive European feudalist striving for the forcible capture of Europe or part of it. On the contrary, he was the first to propose a treaty ensuring the integrity of all European borders. He also "played the Turkish card", but his proposal exceeded the idea of an anti-Turkish coalition; it aimed to safeguard lasting peace in Europe. Obviously, George of Poděbrady aimed at breaking the international isolation of Hussite Bohemia and obtaining some guarantees for the Czech Kingdom. However ambitious he might have been, he did not seem to aspire to a personal position of power in Europe (or in the Byzantine Empire, as some historians suggest). Even in his relations with the Turks he was ahead of his time when he did not discount the possibility of living in peace with them if they gave up invasions.

His "Charter for Europe" of 1464 was the culmination of his impressive international diplomatic activities. In the first part of the "Agreement", he explained the reasons for its origin and submission to European rulers. The second (more profound) part consists of 23 articles outlining possible ways how to protect Europe from military conflicts. It suggests the establishment of a union of states with equal rights that would not interfere with each other's internal affairs and would coordinate their policies using agreed mechanisms and common bodies, such as, for example, the council of rulers (consilium), the international court (consistorium - parlamentum, which presupposed the formulation of generally effective legal standards) and the general assembly of representatives of the Estates-General (congregatio). It also suggests practical solutions to questions of procedures, funding, etc. Louis XI, a French king who was the first to be offered this plan, with a flattering offer to become the leader of the European union, politely declined George's initiative in order to avoid a conflict with Pius II, the Pope, who flatly rejected the plan of his Czech heretic opponent. The legacy of George of Poděbrady has survived through the ages and present-day international organizations such as the UN, the EU, or the Council of Europe can undoubtedly be regarded as the heirs of the ideas of this Czech king.

The Peace League of George Podebrad, King of Bohemia. Prague 1919.

Návrh krále Jiřího na utvoření Svazu evropských států [King George's Proposal on Forming a Union of European States]. Praha 1940.

Eine Weltfriedensorganisation nach den Vorschlägen des böhmischen Königs Georg von Podiebrad und nach den Ideen des Johannes Amos Comenius. Berlin 1963.

The Universal Peace Organization of King George of Bohemia, a Fifteenth-Century Plan for World Peace 1462-1464. Prague 1964.

Všeobecná mírová organizace podle návrhu českého krále Jiřího z let 1462-1464 [Universal Peace Organisation as Proposed by the Czech King George from the Years 1462-1464]. Praha 1967.

KANT IMMANUEL

* 1724 Königsberg   † 1804 Königsberg

"For states and their mutual relations, there cannot exist any other reasonable way how to escape from the illegal situation that implies only wars than the one saying that states - like individual people - will give up their wild (illegal) liberty, subject to public coercive laws, and thus establish a community of nations (which will obviously grow in time) that will finally include all the nations on the earth."

• representative of classical German philosophy • whole life spent in his native city • influenced by his mother (a pietist) - respect for religion and its ethical norms • 1740 studies of theology and philosophy at Königsberg University • from 1755 senior lecturer, later Professor of logic and metaphysics at Königsberg University • until 1770 focus on natural philosophy, later efforts to overcome the weak points of rationalism • development of his own philosophical system • introduction of the category of a generally binding moral law - "a categorical imperative" •

Kant published his plan for eternal peace at the age of 71. He based it on the ideas of the Abbé de Saint-Pierre and J. J. Rousseau, which had attracted him a long time before. In a number of his works written before the Great French Revolution, the concept of "The United Nations" and its essential principles appeared. Kant reasoned that the "antisocial tendencies" of states (taxes, armament, conquest, wars) could not be stopped unless their rulers were deprived of absolute power, which should be given to the nations themselves. He was convinced that wars were not inevitable. His work "Perpetual Peace" was written in the form of an international agreement with six introductory, three "definitive", and two additional articles, in which he formulates the ideas of European federalism. These ideas became the subjects of extensive polemics in the Europe of that time, especially in Germany.

K věčnému míru [Towards Everlasting Peace]. Pardubice, date unknown.

Der ewige Friede. Leipzig 1838-1842.

O svazu národů [On the Union of Nations]. Brno 1924.

O výchově [On Education]. Praha 1931.

Idea všeobecných dějin ve světoobčanském ohledu [The Idea of General History from a Cosmopolitan View]. Praha 1990.

Schriften zur Anthropologie, Geschichtsphilosophie, Politik und Pädagogik. Darmstadt 1998.

Werke. Hamburg 2000.

Basic Writings of Kant. New York 2001.

KEYSERLING HERMANN VON

* 1880 Könno   † 1946 Innsbruck

"A European, and the whole of Europe with him, inevitably originates from an internally experienced, long-existing feeling of integrity as a special product of differentiation. It originates from the feeling of dissimilarity between the East and the West, of which, in the collective awareness of Europeans, what joins them outweighs what divides them. ... Is 'a European' the most perfect man now? Certainly, an appropriate 'supranationalism' will soon appear and must become as virulent as any nationalism has ever been; that would thus represent a European equivalent of Messianic Americanism. But a European, naturally, is a long way from an ideal person, too... ."

• German philosopher • from the Baltic region • studies of natural sciences • understanding of philosophy as a general approach to life and the art of living • 1910-1911 journey round the world • paradigm of the worldly wisdom of the Orient • in 1920 founder and financier of the "School of Wisdom" in Darmstadt • author of aesthetic essays •

In his "Travel Diary of a Philosopher", Keyserling presented "a spectral analysis" of Europe, to which he attributed the task of the spiritual salvation of the whole of mankind. He declared the end of the supremacy of Europe and the ongoing development of the technical and material powers of other continents. In this situation, he saw a necessity for self-preservation in Europe's focusing on something that cannot be taken away from it - on its spirit. According to him, a European embodies a special synthesis of spirit, soul, and body.

For him, as for Ortega y Gasset, for example, establishing a European union was a logical and rightful consequence of what was then the already long-lasting common European existence and spirit. To him, Europeans seemed, under the pressure of non-European peoples, increasingly to realize how many things joined them and how few things divided them, and so their relation to the European entity was undergoing an essential change. He was probably the first to use the term European "supranationality" but he did not deduce from it any necessity for national levelling. The internal contrasts in Europe, in comparison with other continents, seemed to be relative and he reasoned that they functioned as a mutual enrichment within the European entity.

Keyserling regarded celebrating one's own nation at the expense of others as absurd; according to him, patriotism was the "last refuge of scoundrels" and the national way was a road leading from "humanism to bestiality". He saw a possible danger in the rise of "European supranationalism" and therefore he emphasized that Europeanism could not be in any contradiction with the effort for global human harmony. Repeatedly, he pointed out that Europe, in which no movement could subordinate spirit to material being for ever, had great expectations for the future; it advanced the rest of the world psychologically and its spirituality qualifies Europe for an important world role.

Das Reisentagebuch eines Philosophen. Darmstadt 1922.
Die neuenstehende Welt. Darmstadt 1926.
Europe. London 1928.
Analyse spectrale de l'Europe. Paris 1931.
Das Spektrum Europas. Stuttgart 1931.

KOHL HELMUT

* 1930 Ludwigshafen

"Not only the division of Germany but also the division of the continent has long since become obsolete. Many people from the countries of central, eastern and south-eastern Europe look with high expectations towards a unified Europe and certainly towards Germany. It is in the interest of Germany and all of Europe to provide these people with a perspective. ... We do not want any European superstate. We want a Europe where it is possible to negotiate, a Europe which builds unity out of diversity, a Europe which is dedicated to democratic values, a Europe which respects national identity."

• son of a customs officer • brief military training at the end of WWII • studies at the universities in Frankfurt am Main and Heidelberg • 1958 PhD in philosophy • from 1947 active in CDU youth movement • from 1957 chairman of the CDU fraction in the Rhineland-Westphalia federal state parliament • 1966-1974 chairman of the Rhineland-Westphalia CDU and from May 1969 also the prime minister of Rhineland-Westphalia (at the same time a member of the Federal Parliament, the Bundestag) • from 1964 a member of the all-federal executive committee of the CDU • 1969-1973 deputy chairman and from 1973 federal chairman of the CDU • 1976 chairman of the CDU/CSU faction in the Bundestag and opposition leader • 1982-1998 federal Chancellor •

Beside K. Adenauer, Helmut Kohl is the most significant German politician who helped to build the present form of Europe. Together with F. Mitterand, he systematically organized German-French conciliation. He played a key role in the unification of Germany in 1990. In a short time he managed to persuade the world powers to allow a superfast unification process, and then he successfully finished it with a great personal effort. The unification of Germany, however, was just another step towards European integration for Kohl. His dream was to become the "concluder" of European integration. He considered the European dimension to be Germany's political priority. During his time as the federal Chancellor, Germany gained significance in the solution of international issues. Kohl was absolutely devoted to the idea of European integration, because (just like Adenauer) he wanted Germany to become embedded in the European structures in such a way as to prevent it from starting any new military conflict. He believed that possible German efforts to dominate Europe would be eliminated by creating a European political union. He therefore tirelessly and steadily supported the introduction of a unified European currency (although for Germans this would mean parting with the symbol of their "economic miracle" - the Deutschmark), which he regarded as one of the decisive steps toward achieving this aim.

Aussen- und Sicherheitspolitik. Bonn 1982.
German Policy Today. Bonn 1984.
Reden zu Fragen unserer Zeit. Bonn 1986.
Europe 1992. Bonn 1989.
Reden. Bonn 1989.
Deutschlands Zukunft in Europa. Herford 1990.
Partnerschaft in Freiheit. Partnership in liberty. West Stockbridge 1990.
Reden und Erklärungen zur Deutschlandpolitik. Bonn 1990.
Bilanzen und Perspektiven. Bonn 1992.
Die deutsche Einheit. Bergish Gladbach 1992.
United Germany in a Uniting Europe. Oxford 1992.
První a druhá Evropa [First and Second Europe]. Praha 1995.
Mein Tagebuch 1998-2000. München 2000.

KOMENSKÝ JAN AMOS (COMENIUS)

* 1592 Nivnice   † 1670 Amsterdam

"As we should neither conceal our plans and efforts from one another nor work only for ourselves, I will give an example, as my highest ambition is to announce Christ to all nations. This light must be brought to other nations in the name of our European homeland; therefore we have to unite all of us first. We, Europeans, should be regarded as travellers on one ship. I cannot be silent as I would like to announce that my message may moderate the evil of war, as music full of harmony. ... It is a knot worthy of a divine arbiter, a knot more tangled than the Gordian knot, that I in this work submit to you, men standing at the head of the Christian world, to either untangle it by your skills or sunder with the sword of mutual love. ... What prevents us from joining in one state, subject to the same law? ... We, Europeans, are especially bound to try everything possible to support the salvation of this world. ... As we, Europeans, are the midnight side, the city of a great king, the comfort of all the Earth, as the Israelite church foresaw in their minds and sang with joy. ...

To fulfil this prophecy after all and to really become the comfort of all the Earth, the kingdom of Heaven shows us - Europeans - a new, straight and pleasant path... A path showing one religion instead of so many discordant ones..., instead of so many forms of mutually subverted state executives it shows only one way, so simple and nevertheless so effective for keeping all the people of the world *in peace that no lions or other beasts would appear on that path, if people decided to take it. ... "*

• Czech pedagogue, theologian, philosopher, and writer • 1608-1611 studies at the Brethren's grammar school in Přerov • from 1611 studies of theology in Herborn and Heidelberg • 1616 ordained as a priest • 1618 at the head of the Brethren's Congregation in Fulnek • into hiding after the defeat at the Battle of the White Mountain • 1628 exile • 1628-1641 work in Lešno - writing his essential pedagogical works • teacher, later Rector of the Brethren's grammar school • secretary and archivist of the Church of the Moravian Brethren • 1641-1642 stay in London at the invitation of the English Parliament • 1642-1648 stay in Elblag - work on textbooks • 1648 return to Lešno - the last bishop of the Church of the Moravian Brethren • 1650 stay in Blatenský Potok at the invitation of the Transylvanian Prince - attempt to realize his educational programme • 1654-1656 his last stay in Lešno - his library, manuscripts, and archives of the Church of the Moravian Brethren destroyed by fire • 1656-1670 stay in Amsterdam - culmination of his scholarly and literary work • buried in Naarden •

Comenius' pilgrimage was one of a real European, as he lived and worked in many countries. He observed and experienced for himself the dramatic and tragic events of the 17th century. That influenced his search for a better future not only for the Czech Kingdom but also for Europe and the whole world. During his stay in England, he expressed his thoughts on overall enlightenment and the improvement of human society in his work "The Way of Light". The mystic light is a metaphorical expression for the idea of general progress, the international organization of science, education, and the dissemination of learning. Comenius dreamt of a universal language and planned the establishment of a board of scholars ("collegium lucis") that would, with the peaceful cooperation of European nations, control the universal education of all people from birth up to adulthood.

He continued to think and work in this sense and in the final phase of his life he devoted most of his energy to seeking ways leading to a peaceful organization of the world, and especially Europe. Thus his monumental project came into existence (however not completed):

"General Advice on the Reform of Human Affairs". In seven unequally elaborated parts, he searched for and proposed ways and methods how to reform human society, how to reconcile nations (the Jews and the Turks included). He invited people to a discussion on attitudes and he also formulated principles of democratic political culture. Obviously, he rejected warlike solutions to problems. He proposed authorities that should ensure a general reform: "a congregation of light" (which should clean the light of knowledge), "a holy consistory" (taking care of devotion and decency) and "a court of peace" (which should ensure the civil administration of the world and protect it against the abuse of power). These authorities were to be established in every state and also on each continent, while Europe was allocated the leading role and London would be the seat of "the academy of light, peace, and love". Under the conditions then prevailing, he attributed a special position to "the most powerful trio of northern kingdoms" (Poland, Sweden, and England), symbolizing the three main religious streams.

Comenius' plan was the most utopian project of the four biggest ones that originated in the period between the early 17th and early 18th centuries. However, because of its emphasis on education and morality, it represents an extraordinary stimulus and it shines like a diamond of European thinking even nowadays.

Ausgewählte Schriften zur Reform in Wissenschaft, Religion und Politik. Leipzig 1924.
Apoštol míru J. A. Komenský. Výbor z díla [An Apostle of Peace - J. A. Comenius. Selected Works]. Praha 1949.
Selections from his Works. Prague 1964.
Listy přátelům a příznivcům [Letters to Friends and Supporters]. Praha 1970.
Panglottia, or Universal light. Shipston-on-Stour 1989.
Cesta světla [The Way of Light]. Praha 1992.
Obecná porada o nápravě věcí lidských [General Advice on a Reform of Human Affairs]. Praha 1992.
Panorthosia or Universal Reform. Sheffield 1995.

LAMARTINE ALPHONSE DE

* 1790 Mâcon   † 1869 Paris

"In a loud voice and with deep conviction, we declare that the French Republic will feel authorized to use arms if, as an act of providence, the time for the re-elevation of some European nations which have hitherto been oppressed comes once again. ... Through the light of its ideas, the picture of order and peace the Republic will give to the world, it will summon the world to conversion, to the only sound and honest conversion, to mutual respect and understanding. This kind of behaviour is not aggressive, but natural, as it does not mean rebellion but the awakening of Europe, not setting the world on fire, but throwing a bright light over the horizon of nations; it is supremacy as well as guidance."

• French poet, politician, and historian • studies in Lyon and Belley • travels around Italy • military service up until 1815 • 1825-1828 French chargé d'affaires in Florence • supporter of the July monarchy • 1833 deputy of the National Assembly - soon very popular • 1848 most influential member of the Interim Government • loss of popularity after riots in June • after the coup in 1851 life in seclusion •

Lamartine always glorified the noble role of France, which would bring liberty to Europe. He was convinced that there was no major discord between the European and the French interests. When in February 1848 he became Minister of Foreign Affairs in the revolutionary government, he issued the "Proclamation to Europe", in which he empha-

117

sized the European idea of harmony and unity and he expressed his conviction that the time for bringing to completion the mission of the Great French Revolution had arrived - the time to introduce general brotherhood all over the world. At the same time, he reserved for France the right to use arms to liberate those enslaved European countries which had not yet achieved freedom (namely Switzerland and Italy). In his proclamation, the generally well-known Jacobin ideas of the French "bayonet liberation and unification" of Europe are clearly evident.

A. v. Lamartine's sämmtliche werke. Stuttgart 1843.
Rede vor der Deputiertenkammer 1843. Paris 1843.
Trois mois au pouvoir. Paris 1848.
Über die rationelle Politik. Leipzig 1848.
Die Vergangenheit, Gegenwart und Zukunft der fränzösischen Republik. Stuttgart 1850.
Meditace [Meditation]. Praha 1907.
Gestalten der Revolution. München 1965.
Discours et articles d'Alphonse de Lamartine. Mâcon 1990.
La politique et l'histoire. Paris 1993.

LEIBNIZ GOTTFRIED WILHELM

* 1646 Leipzig   † 1716 Hanover

"I do not belong among those who fanatically stick to their homeland or even to a particular nation; I am for service to all mankind, as I regard the heavens as my homeland and all kind people are my fellow-citizens in these heavens; and I would rather do a lot of good among the Russians than merely a little among the Germans or other Europeans. ... My sympathies and my pleasure are directed at the common good."

• German philosopher, lawyer, mathematician, and diplomat • 1661-1666 studies of law, philosophy, and mathematics at Leipzig and Jena Universities • 1666 Doctorate in Law at Nürnberg University • 1667-1672 work at the University in Frankfurt am Main and in Mainz - writing theological, philosophical, legal, and political works • 1672-1676 study trip Paris-London-the Netherlands - meeting and corresponding with renowned scientists and scholars (R. Bayle, I. Newton, B. Spinoza) • 1676-1716 librarian and counsel at the Hanover court • 1700 first president of the Academy of Science in Berlin • contacts with royal courts in Berlin, Vienna, and St. Petersburg • 1711 appointed a court counsel • scientific successes in philosophy, physics, linguistics, and legal sciences •

During the course of his life, Leibniz got to know the majority of European countries; he admired the diversity of their cultures and was concerned about their disputes, which is why he was looking for ways to bring about the unification of Europe (and all the world). He submitted a federalist project dealing with this matter to Louis XIV. His proposal, "Consilium Aegyptianorum", tried to direct the French monarch's ambitions towards the Orient, thereby lessening tension in Europe so that at a later date European unity might be achieved. (At first, his proposal attracted the king, who even invited Leibniz to Paris, but eventually he did not receive him because, in the meantime, he had come to an agreement with the Turkish Sultan.)

Although he was a Lutheran, he also admired Catholicism and he hoped for a reconciliation of all religions in the ecumenical sense (he even proposed cooperation with the Jesuits). Like Dante, he accentuated the historical role of the papacy, which, along with the kaisership, had provided Europe with stability. (Consequently, he also appreciated a proposal by the Hessian Prince to establish a "European Catholic Court" in Lucerne, which should be presided over by the Pope.)

Leibniz tried to find a universal means that could be used for communication throughout the continent. He strove to establish new universities around Europe and to unite them in a large European Academy of Scholars. Leibniz considered himself not only a European but also a cosmopolitan and his final goal was a global synthesis. Being an adviser to Peter the Great, he had hopes for Russia as a link connecting Europe and Asia. At the end of the 17th century, he published a text, "The State of Affairs in Europe at the Beginning of a New Century", full of his conviction that European affairs would show a different face at the end of the 18th century.

Nouveaux essais sur l'entendement humain. 1704.
Nové úvahy o lidské soudnosti od autora systému předzjednané harmonie [New Considerations of Human Insight by the Author of the System of Pre-Arranged Harmony]. Praha 1932.
Fragmente zur Logik. Berlin 1960.
Monadologie a jiné práce [Monadology and other Works]. Praha 1982.
Philosophische Schriften und Briefe 1683-1687. Berlin 1992.
New Essays on Human Understanding. Cambridge 1996.
Philosophische Schriften. Frankfurt a. M. 1996.

MADARIAGA Y RUJO SALVATOR

* 1886 La Coruña   † 1978 Locarno

"The supremacy of mind and will and the close kinship between these two abilities in European psychology explain why the traditions of Socrates and Christianity are the strongest European traditions. Socrates dominates the mind of Europe, Jesus its will. ... It is useless to ask whether these two traditions are the origin or the result of the European character, as they are both the origin and the result, the cause and influence, and, which means even more, by their close unification of the mind and will, they influenced each other in a natural way to such an extent that, through centuries of European life, Christ has become a Socrates and Socrates has become a Christ. ... Europe adheres to both liberty and quality. ... All life is valuable and therefore, in Europe, we must protect ourselves from both the menaces which threaten our lives, from both the antipodes of value: quantity and uniformity."*

• Spanish politician and journalist • studies at Paris Polytechnic and University • 1916-1921 London - work for the Times - first works published • 1921-1938 officer of the Press Bureau, later in the Disarmament Department of the United Nations • 1928-1930 Head of the Department of Spanish literature at Oxford University • 1931 return to Spain - elected to the National Assembly • 1931 appointed ambassador in Washington • 1932-1934 ambassador in Paris • 1932-1936 at the same time representative of Spain in the United Nations • 1934 Minister of Education and Justice in the Leroux government • on outbreak of the Civil War return to Oxford University • from 1954 lecture stays in numerous countries •

As a liberal, Madariaga (like Benedetto Croce, another father of liberalism) united the concept of Europe primarily with the idea of liberty (e. g. in his work "The Spirit of Europe"). He perceived liberty as the decisive form of existence and "the essence of life" in Europe, inseparably linked with liberalism in human affairs. He emphasized the quality and variety of forms of European life, characterized by its rejection of uniformity. European culture radiates outwardly; as the spirit and the will of Europeans are in balance, this harmony results in the valuable activity and creation of the Europeans. The spirit and the will are based on the unmistakable character of individuals and Europe is the most individualistic and least conformist continent of all. In Europe, "the individual is king", and this conditions the activity of the European spirit. While, for an American, knowledge is a tool for negotiations and business and, for an Indian, a medium of self-liberation, for a European, knowledge is a way that leads to the conquest of nature. Europe even has a strange life rhythm: after the first period, the will governing the spirit leads directly to its goal, and after the second, when the spirit rules the will, a third period comes, in which a balance of will and spirit leads to a synthesis. This three-phase cycle applies in scientific work, political activities, and in the development of law, as well as in the international functioning of Europe. When examining the profile of Europe, Madariaga refused to make a preference between classical or Christian influences, but instead saw them as complementary.

Angličané, Francouzi, Španělé. Rozbor národních povah [The English, the French, the Spanish. An Analysis of National Characters]. Praha 1931.
The Future of International Government. Oxford 1941.
Europe, a Unit of Human Culture. Brussels 1952.
Europa, eine kulturelle Einheit. Brüssel 1952.
L'Esprit de l'Europe. Bruxelles 1952.
Portrait de l'Europe. Paris 1952.
Porträt Europas. Stuttgart 1952.
Portrait of Europe. London 1967.
Carácter y destino en Europa. Madrid 1980.

Maistre Joseph Marie de

* 1753 Chambery † 1821 Turin

"The greatest enemy of Europe, which must be removed by any possible means, excluding criminal acts, is a sore bringing about total destruction, which attaches itself to every sovereign power and unceasingly festers, the son of pride, the father of anarchy, a mighty annihilator - Protestantism."

• Italian diplomat and writer • studies of law at Turin University • court official • from 1788 senator in Savoy • after the French invasion in 1792 forced to leave for Lausanne - journalistic activities • from 1793 service at the court of the Sardinian king • 1802-1817 ambassador in St. Petersburg • 1817 return to Turin - appointed a royal minister •

Although Maistre was of French extraction, he was one of the most fanatical adversaries of the Great French Revolution in all its forms. He resisted Napoleon and rejected nationalism as well as democracy. He believed that Europe was standing at the pinnacle of human history but at the same time he viewed its future with profound pessimism. He viewed the only hope for salvation in a "return of the nations back to Rome" and in unconditional subordination to the Pope, who he saw as the creator of all culture, the founder of the European monarchies, and the source of European morality.

He rejected any reconciliation with Protestantism or Orthodoxy and indeed, on the contrary, fulminated against them and called for their unconditional surrender to the Vatican. He was probably the most extreme advocate of the unification of Europe under the restored and extended power of Catholicism.

Abendstunden zu St. Petersburg oder Gespräche über das Walten der göttlichen Vorsicht in zeitlichen Dingen, mit einem über die Opfer. Frankfurt a. M. 1824.

Correspondance diplomatique de Joseph de Maistre, 1811-1817. Paris 1860.

Mémoires politiques et correspondance diplomatique. Paris 1864.

Oeuvres. Du pape précédé d'un avant propos et suivi de la constitution Pastor Aeternus. Arras 1874.

Plan d'un nouvel équilibre en Europe. Tours 1881.

Oeuvres complètes de J. de Maistre. Lyon 1884-1893.

Vom Papste. München 1923.

Betrachtungen über Frankreich. Berlin 1924.

The Works of Joseph de Maistre. London 1965.

Essay on the Generative Principle of Political Constitutions. Boston 1981.

Il pensiero politico di De Maistre. Roma 1993.

MARX KARL HEINRICH

* 1818 Trier † 1883 London

"The Nations of the West will once again rise to power and to common goals. Russia, however, will be broken by the progress of the masses and by explosive force. ... The fall of the bourgeoisie in France, the triumph of the French working class, the emancipation of the working class itself, this is the motto of the French liberation. ... Workers of the world, unite!"

• German philosopher, economist, and politician • 1830-1835 grammar school in Trier • 1835-1841 studies of law, philosophy, and history at Bonn, Berlin, and Jena Universities • 1842-1843 editor-in-chief of the "Rheinische Zeitung" - beginning of cooperation with F. Engels • 1843 editor of the "Deutsch-französische Jahrbücher" magazine in Paris • 1845-1848 stay in Brussels • 1847 member of the "Union of the Right-Minded" - charged with elaborating the programme together with Engels • 1848 "Communist Manifesto" • 1848 return to Germany - editor of the "Neue Rheinische Zeitung" • exile in 1849, departure from Germany for London - publication of his essential works • 1864 co-founder and secretary of the First International •

Throughout his life, Marx shared the opinion of Hegel, his teacher of philosophy, that Western Europe was the most progressive part of the world and was therefore competent to shape the future of mankind. According to him, the unification of Europe could be ensured neither by members of the liberal bourgeoisie nor by idealists such as Mazzini (who he mocked), but only by the proletariat. Bourgeois England, transformed by revolution, was to stand at the head of the European revolutionary movement. European unification would also have to be supported by the USA.

Marx saw a permanent danger for Europe in Russia, which represented the threat of world-ruling "Mongolian barbarism". Like Engels, he welcomed the anti-Russian rebellion of the oppressed Polish nation. He saw the end of Russian feudal expansive tendencies in "the progress of the masses" and in socialist revolution.

Class struggle, the historic role of the united proletariat, and the socialist revolution under Communist leadership - these were the basic ideas of Marx's path towards a united Europe - Europe under the dictatorship of the proletariat.

Osmnáctý brumaire Ludvíka Bonaparta [The 18th Brumaire of Louis Bonaparte].
    Praha 1949.
The Russian Menace to Europe. Glencoe 1952.
La Russie et l'Europe. Paris 1954.
The Revolutions of 1848. Baltimore 1973.
Ekonomicko-filozofické rukopisy [Economical-Philosophical Manuscripts].
    Praha 1978.
Kapitál I.-III. [The Capital I-III]. Praha 1986-1989.
Manifest komunistické strany [Manifesto of the Communist Party]. Praha 1988.
Political Writings. London 1992.

MASARYK JAN

* 1886 Prague † 1948 Prague

"I am often asked what I think about European federation. I am all for it... A nation state focused on itself, which never existed anyway, has become a matter of the past. ... All nations, small as well as big ones, must voluntarily give up a part of their sovereignty to achieve that common goal..., I often spoke with my father about small nations. ... We disagreed over one matter. He believed that small nations, such as for example us Czechs, should be like bridges between those big ones. I have never liked that idea very much. Bridges are for treading on. ... Neither a curtain, nor a bridge, but a link in a democratic chain that surrounds the world and binds this earth together."

• Czechoslovak politician and diplomat • 1906 graduation from Academic Grammar School in Prague • 1907-1913 stay in Chicago • 1914-1918 reserve officer in the Austrian army • 1919 entry into the diplomatic service of the Czechoslovak Republic • 1919-1920 chargé d'affaires in Washington • 1921-1925 work at the Ministry of Foreign Affairs in Prague • 1925-1938 Ambassador in London • 1939 departure from London for the U.S.A. • 1940 return to London - Minister of Foreign Affairs in the Czechoslovak government in exile • participation in the establishment of the Czechoslovak army abroad • 1945-1948 Minister of Foreign Affairs of the Czechoslovak Republic •

In European politics, Jan Masaryk acted in the spirit of the vision of his father Tomáš Garrigue Masaryk and his successor E. Beneš. He

127

achieved great popularity and had numerous diplomatic successes in Europe, but nevertheless clung to certain illusions (e. g. about the Soviet Union, along with Beneš) and remained somewhat credulous (e. g. towards domestic communists). He enthusiastically supported all ideas of democratic international cooperation and warmly welcomed the birth of the United Nations Organization, as a platform for the restoration of international law. That is why he was, in 1946, elected the first chairman of the "World Federation of an Association for the United Nations". He fully identified himself with the idea of a European federation and devoted a great deal of attention to the idea, especially during World War II. He understood it as a guarantee against the repetition of all Europe's pre-war evils, and especially as a guarantee against chauvinism, which had helped bring about the war. He supported the idea of a Czech-Polish confederation not only as a security organ, but also as one of the cornerstones of the building of a united Europe. He initially supported Beneš' idea of the Czechoslovak Republic as a bridge between the West and the East, but later abandoned it. His well-known optimism helped him survive the turmoil connected with the break-up of the Allies during the war period, along with the gradual creation of the Iron Curtain, issues related to the Marshall Plan in Moscow, and the events of February 1948. Inside himself, however, he sank deeper and deeper into despair, which probably led to the tragic end of his life.

Das Problem der kleinen Völker in der europäischen Krisis. Praha 1922.
A Free Czechoslovakia and a Free Germany, in a Free Europe. Westminster 1939.
Československá zahraniční politika [Czechoslovak Foreign Policy]. Praha 1947.
Ani opona, ani most [Neither a Curtain nor a Bridge]. Praha 1951.
Volá Londýn [London Calling]. Praha 1990.

Masaryk Tomáš Garrigue

* 1850 Hodonín   † 1937 Lány

"… mankind fights for unity but not for uniformity: a world federation, not world supremacy, consensus gentium, not the slavery of nations and races; the organization, not the conquest of Europe. Not a Herrenvolk, but equality among nations. … A new human being, homo europaeus, will not come about merely through an external policy, but mostly through an internal one… . The political task of the democratic reconstruction of Europe must be completed and actually enabled by the moral re-education of nations. … Jesus, not Caesar - this is the motto of a democratic Europe… ."

• Czech philosopher, politician, and statesman • 1865-1869 German Grammar School in Brno • 1869-1872 Academic Grammar School in Vienna • 1872-1876 studies of philosophy and classical languages at Vienna University • 1876 Doctorate in Philosophy • 1876-1877 publication of first scientific works • 1879-1882 Senior lecturer in philosophy at Vienna University • 1882-1914 Professor of the Czech University of Prague • editor of the "Atheneum" journal • 1891-1893 delegate for the Radical Democrats in the Czech Assembly and Imperial Council • 1900 co-founder of the Czech People's Party (The Realistic Party) • 1907-1914 delegate to the Imperial Council • 1914 departure for exile - vision of a national independence programme • negotiations on Czech and Slovak national self-determination in England, France, and the USA • organizer of the Czechoslovak legion • 1917 stay in Russia • 1918-1935 the first President of Czechoslovakia •

In many aspects, Masaryk built upon Palacky's approach to the Czech nation and Europe; he considered the equality of nations as a necessary precondition for the democratic federalization of Europe, with a special emphasis on the territory of Central Europe. If he was the executor of the historical verdict on Austria-Hungary, he performed the role in full awareness of the necessity to look for new and more equal European coalitions. A modest evidence of his approach was the Little Entente or the unsuccessful attempt (made within the Paris peace negotiations) to establish "The United States of Eastern Europe", which would have associated the states between Russia and Germany into a federation. For Masaryk, the final goal was always the unification of all Europe. He therefore conspicuously supported the Coudenhove-Kalergi Pan-European Movement. As early as during World War I, he expressed the conviction that the post-war organization of Europe would have to be based on democratic and just principles so that the newly-born peaceful Europe would be free of the germs of new conflicts. He incorporated his ideas into his work "The New Europe", in which he supported the principle of the national self-determination of nations and their complete equality, as well as their unification not in supranational forms but in an association of democratic nations, because democracy and humanism did not, in his view, have any borders. He rejected secret diplomacy and called for general disarmament, for the establishment of a pan-European market, and even for "A Union of Nations". This Union would even have included Russia and the process of uniting mankind would not have stopped at the borders of our continent.

Masaryk's European prestige was so high that G. B. Shaw stated that if a president for a united Europe were to be sought, there could be found no more suitable candidate than Masaryk.

Otázka sociální [Social Issue]. Praha 1898.
Russland und Europa. Jena 1913.
The New Europe. London 1918.
Nová Evropa [New Europe]. Praha 1920.
Slované po válce [The Slavs after the War]. Praha 1923.
Svět a Slované [The World and the Slavs]. Praha 1924.

Světová revoluce [World Revolution]. Praha 1925.

Problém malých národů v evropské krisi [Problem of Small Nations in the European Crisis]. Praha 1926.

The Slavs and their Place in Europe. Glasgow 1928.

Rusko a Evropa [Russia and Europe]. Praha 1932.

Palackého idea národa českého [Palacky's Idea of the Czech Nation]. Praha 1947.

Ideály humanitní [Humanist Ideals]. Praha 1968.

The Ideals of Humanity and How to Work. New York 1971.

Česká otázka [The Czech Issue]. Praha 1990.

O demokracii [On Democracy]. Praha 1991.

MAZZINI GIUSEPPE

* 1805 Genoa   † 1872 Pisa

"Yes, only in ourselves can we find the exact reason for this (failure in the attempt to unite Europe by revolutionary means), in lack of organization, in the disintegration of our order... in the lack of confidence, in our permanent petty vanities. ... in the waste of our strength in innumerable small local struggles, groups, sects, and blocks, whose powers are manifested in the trampling down of everything without building anything new."

• Italian politician, revolutionary, representative of the Republican wing of the Italian unification movement • studies of law in Genoa • 1827-1830 member of Carbonari secret societies - arrest and imprisonment • 1831 anti-monarchist plan for Italian unification • 1831 departure for Switzerland and France • founder of the "Young Italy" society and author of its programme • preparing revolution in Sardinia - conspiracy was disclosed, sentenced to death in absentia • 1834 co-founder of the "Young Europe" movement in Geneva • exile from Switzerland due to pressure from the Great Powers • 1837 London • return to Italy when the revolution began in 1848 - Lombardy, Rome • 1849 participation in the establishment of the Roman Republic - elected as triumvir • after French intervention escape to England • co-founder of the "European Committee" - programme of pan-European politics • 1870 return to Italy •

Metternich used to say that Mazzini was as eloquent as a storm, as amusing as a comedian, and as untiring as a man in love, but also a danger for all Europe. Mazzini was almost mystically devoted to the most high-minded ideals of the time; he believed in liberty, love, and harmony among nations. The republican idea of a united Italy led him to the idea of a united Europe, the groundwork of which should have been created by the united monarchies of Italy, Austria, and France. He inspired the founding of the "Young Italy", "Young Germany", "Young France", and "Young Switzerland" societies. These societies, along with others from all European countries, were supposed to liberate and unite all of Europe. In 1848, this integration vision seemed to be close at hand. Shortly after, however, human liberties were chained once again, nationalism triumphed over understanding among nations, and Mazzini could only analyze the reasons behind this failure. He assigned it, in the first place, to the insufficient readiness for action of the European federalists themselves.

De l'initiative révolutionnaire en Europe. Paris 1835.
Foi et Avenir. Paris 1850.
The Revolutionary Initiative of the Peoples. London 1852.
Coup d'état européen. Londres 1859.
Opere. Mailand 1861.
Essays. London 1887.
Úvahy, vybrané z literárních, politických a náboženských spisů Josefa Mazziniho [Reflections Selected from Literary, Political and Religious Works of Giuseppe Mazzini]. Praha 1900.
La jeune Italie et la jeune Europe. Paris 1908.
Italia ed Europa. Roma 1945.
Thoughts upon Democracy in Europe. Firenze 2001.

MITTERAND FRANÇOIS

* 1916 Jarnac † 1996 Paris

"Europe needs a horizon, she needs a working method, she needs the ambition to mobilize, she needs immediate appropriate action. ... Space is required for new European institutions. I firmly believe that Europe can gain a perspective on her diversity; otherwise she would remain very frail. First we need a European community; a very strong and very compact community. I am one of those who aim at an economic, monetary, and political union. I do not visualize a confederacy to achieve estrangement. ... Let us simply state that we need very flexible structures, limited in such a way as to avoid the mass return of bureaucracy, which would, in itself, be very burdensome."

• French left-wing politician • studies of philosophy and law at university • mixed fortunes during WWII: capture by the Germans, escape, cooperation with the Vichy puppet government, then engagement in the resistance movement • 1944 member of de Gaulle's provisional government - after the war a minister several times (e. g. Minister of the Interior, Minister of Justice) • 1946-1958 and 1962-1981 member of the House of Representatives • 1959-1962 Senator • 1965 first candidature for presidency, against de Gaulle • 1971-1980 Secretary-General of the Socialist Party • from 1981 President of France for 14 years (the first socialist president in French history): elected three times (the longest presidential term of service in French history since Napoleon III) •

As regards Mitterand's domestic policy, it is worth recalling his effort to implement social programmes, to nationalize banks and key industries, and to abolish the death sentence. But from the European point of view, his foreign policy activities, especially within the European Community, are the most important. He tried to strengthen and consolidate German-French relations and he found a partner in Chancellor Kohl, who had the same objectives. Under their leadership, Franco-German co-operation became the motor of European integration in the 1980s and at the beginning of the 1990s (although, at the same time, he attempted to strengthen the French nuclear forces). The aim of Mitterand's foreign policy was to permanently join the destiny of united Germany with that of Europe, and that was why he did his best to build up a political union. The first step was to create a monetary union, which he - with German support - actually managed to enforce by the Maastricht treaty. Under Mitterand's government, France reinforced her position on the European continent, but at the same time she increased her pro-European involvement.

Sur l'Europe: allocution prononcée le 9 mai 1991, à l'occasion de la remise du prix Charlemagne. La Tour d'Aigues 1991.

Projet de Confédération européenne en Histoire de la construction européenne. Paris 1993.

De l'Allemagne, de la France. Paris 1996.

Réflexions sur la politique extérieure de la France. Introduction à vingt discours. Paris 1996.

MONNET JEAN

* 1888 Cognac   † 1979 Montfort-l'Amaury

"In Europe, there will never be peace, as long as European countries are constituted on the basis of national sovereignty. European countries are too small to provide their citizens with the necessary wealth and social development. Therefore, European countries must join into a federation. ..."

• French political economist and diplomat • 1919-1923 deputy of the Secretary-General of the League of Nations • from 1925 work in an investment bank • at the beginning of WWII chairman of the French-British economic coordinating committee • 1940 departure to the USA • 1943 cooperation with de Gaulle in Algeria • after the liberation of France head of the government committee for the reconstruction and modernization of the French economy • 1947 "Monnet's plan" adopted by the French government and Monnet charged with managing the National Planning Committee • 1950 initiation, together with Robert Schuman, of the introduction of a common European market for coal and steel • 1952-1955 president of the European Coal and Steel Community • 1956-1975 president of the Action Committee of the United States of Europe • 1976 named "European citizen" by representatives of governments from the European Economic Community •

This French politician is often referred to as the "Father of Europe", because, without him, the European Communities would probably never have come into existence. He entered international politics after WWI and he believed that the moral power of the League of Nations would lead to a termination of conflicts between countries and nations. However, he soon learned that the opposite would be true, and that the power of veto frustrated his desire to empower general supranational interests. During WWII, in London, he first proposed the formation of an Anglo-French federal union. This proposal found supporters both in Churchill and de Gaulle. Immediately after the liberation of France, Monnet became the commissioner for the reconstruction of the French economy. He soon comprehended that this reconstruction could not take place without a concurrent reconstruction of Germany, where it was necessary to neutralize German militaristic tendencies. Monnet came to the conclusion that the best solution would be common control over strategic raw materials, such as coal and steel. He therefore proposed to the French Minister of Foreign Affairs, Robert Schuman, that control over these branches of industry should be handed over to common European institutions. Schuman accepted these proposals and included them in his declaration, which he presented on 9 May 1950. One year later, the Treaty of Paris was signed, on the basis of which the European Coal and Steel Community (ECSC) was founded, exactly according to Monnet's ideas. In 1955, there was a serious European crisis when the French Parliament refused to ratify the European Defence Community, which was supposed to complement the ECSC. Monnet immediately founded the action committee of the United States of Europe, whose function was to remind European elites of the need for European integration and unification. He continued tirelessly in this activity until his death. Although Monnet did not have a leading political function, he nevertheless managed to enforce his vision of the post-war arrangement of Europe. Without him, Europe would not be the Europe we know today. It was he who enforced the integration principle and who outlined the basic institutions of the integration structures. His principle consisted of a certain succession - first to establish common structures in certain areas, then to expand them to other areas. Gradually, national sovereignty in individual areas was to be transferred to supranational institutions. This method is often described as functionalistic, because its individual steps are not objectives in themselves but lead to the achievement of the final objective. This objective was an integrated and united Europe, whose nations could not enter wars any more simply because of the fact that they shared common supranational interests. Monnet's vision was simultaneously both very flexible and elitist, because he did not believe that the general public could comprehend the meaning of his efforts. Therefore, he tried to achieve his aims in political negotiations, where he persuaded European statesmen about the rightness of his conceptions.

Erinnerungen eines Europäers. 1978.
Repères pour une méthode. Paris 1996.
Mémoires. Paris 1997.

Montesquieu Secondat Charles-Louis de

* 1689 La Brède   † 1755 Paris

"The situation in Europe is characterized by the mutual dependence of all states upon one another. France needs the wealth of Poland and Russia, as Guyenne needs Brittany and Brittany needs the Anjou province. Europe is a state of a number of provinces. ... This is the reason why Europe dominates the rest of the world, prospers, and develops, since its arts prosper and develop, while the rest of the world groans in the fetters of slavery and misery. ... If I knew about something that would be useful for me, but harmful for my family, I would put it out of my mind; if I knew about something that would be useful for my family but not for my homeland, I would forget it as soon as possible. And if I knew about something that would be useful for my homeland but harmful for Europe and all mankind, I would regard it as a crime."

• philosopher, historian, and writer of the French Enlightenment • studies of law at Bordeaux University • office of Royal Court Presiding Judge in Bordeaux • focus on science and travel • 1721 successful satire on French society in his "Persian Letters" • 1721 arrival in Paris - scientific and literary works • 1728-1731 study stay in Germany, Hungary (Slovak mining towns), Italy, and England • 1748 his greatest work "On The Spirit of Laws" - criticism of despotism, inspiring the authors of the first French constitution •

In his reviews of Europe (to be found in, for example, his "Persian Letters", "On the Spirit of Laws", and "On the Powers of the State") Montesquieu made use of the wide experience gathered from his own observations. Although he was an extraordinarily brave critic of the situation in Europe, at the same time he saw a number of aspects which made Europe superior, in comparison with other continents. He found the explanation in the development of sciences and the atmosphere of liberty, which was gradually improving. He explained the differences among Asian nations in terms of energy, laziness, effeminacy, or strength, by the existence of a wide range of climatic zones, while stating that the temperate European climate supports equality in terms of wealth, power, liberty, and mutual respect and coherence among European nations. In his opinion, Europe was the workshop of mankind with its spirit of liberty predestined to take a historical role throughout the whole world.

Montesquieu was, at the same time, a determined pacifist and rejecter of nationalism and privileges of any kind, and thus his complimentary assessment of Europe by no means aimed at encouraging the European conquest of the world.

Oeuvres complètes de Montesquieu. Oxford 1900.
O duchu zákonů [On the Spirit of Laws]. Praha 1947.
Perské listy [Persian Letters]. Praha 1989.
Réflexions sur la monarchie universelle en Europe. Genève 2000.

MÜLLER JOHANNES VON

* 1752 Schaffhausen   † 1809 Kassel

"European policy seems to be more elaborate and more persistent. In the policy of the Orient, on the other hand, the instant energy is obvious. Nowadays, we find ourselves in the midst of a drama that was induced by the giants of the North, the annihilators of the old Empire."

• Swiss historian • studies of theology and history at Göttingen University • 1772-1780 tutor in Geneva • 1781-1783 lectures at the Carl College in Kassel • 1783-1785 work in Geneva and Bern • 1785-1788 librarian and counsel in Mainz • from 1788 holder of high state offices at the court • after French occupation of Mainz in 1797, departure for Vienna - appointed Privy Councillor in the court office • dissatisfied with local conditions; departure for Berlin - historiographer at the court of Frederick II • 1806 called on by Napoleon - appointed a state secretary • 1807 sent to the Westphalian kingdom - Minister of Education • disappointed by political developments - return to Switzerland •

During the period when this famous Swiss historian served in Austrian or Prussian institutions, he rejected the idea of the supremacy of one state in Europe. As soon as he became a minister of the Westphalian King, Napoleon's brother, he radically changed his opinions and called for the removal of the old forms of European structure and their replacement by a new (Napoleonic) order.

141

In his imposing scientific work on European history, he came to the gloomy conclusion that Europe was faced with decay, and he saw the future in Russia or America. Having completed comparative analyses of the cultures of Europe and other continents, he came to a general thesis about the European connection with the rest of the world, especially with the Orient.

Johannes von Müllers sämmtliche Werke. Tübingen 1835.
24 Bücher Allgemeiner Geschichten, besonders der europäischen Menschheit. Stuttgart 1840.
The History of the World. New York 1855.
Geschichte Schweizerischer Eidgenossenschaft. Zürich 1942.
Allgemeine Aussicht über die Bundesrepublik im Schweizerland. Zürich 1991.
Vue générale de la République Fédérative des Suisses. Zürich 1991.

NIETZSCHE FRIEDRICH

* 1844 Röcken   † 1900 Weimar

"Europe, at present, is the scene of an absurdly rapid attempt at a radical blending of walks of life and consequently races. It is therefore skeptical in all heights and depths - with either vacillating skepticism which jumps from one branch to another or murky as a cloud fraught with question marks - and over-saturated to death with its own will! The paralysis of the will: we find this cripple in so many places! And how dressed up he is! How seductively dressed up!"

• German philosopher • 1865 studies of philology at Bonn and Leipzig Universities • 1869 Professor of classical philology at Basel University • 1879 pensioned off for health reasons • stays in Germany, Switzerland, and Italy • 1879-1889 scientific work • 1889 serious mental illness - termination of his works - death •

The end of Nietzsche's life comes simultaneously with the end of the 19th century, which he regarded as a catastrophic time for Europe. When admiring Europe, he tended to mention chiefly the periods of Ancient Greece and the Renaissance, while the contemporary era seemed to him chaotic and heading for the worst. He admitted, however, that this "plebeian and half-barbarian period" might later, after having been suffered through, bring a spiritual success ("the raising of a new caste ruling Europe").

He characterized nationalism as an outgrowth of the Romanticism to which Europe had succumbed, and denounced the unhealthy disaffection that the "national madness" brought and would further disseminate among nations. He insisted that if the great European figures of that century (e.g. Napoleon, Goethe, Beethoven, Heine, Wagner) were subject to patriotism, they were "only having a rest from themselves", as the permanent direction of their souls and their work was defined by their efforts to achieve a new European national synthesis and the formation of a "good European man" for the future.

Nietzsche forecast the necessity for the political and cultural unification of Europe, as well as the introduction of a common market. He warned that delays in European integration due to lack of will and power could turn Russia into the historical winner. When asked whether Europe would still be able to fulfil its mission in the 20th century, he answered - "probably yes". He eventually became more and more pessimistic in his visions; the "hammer of philosophy" was the last weapon available for "good Europeans"; they had better prefer death to mediocrity!

Tak pravil Zarathustra [Thus Spake Zarathustra]. Praha 1967.
Nečasové úvahy [Outmoded Considerations]. Praha 1992.
Ecce homo. Praha 1993.
Der Wille zur Macht. Stuttgart 1996.
Von Nutzen und Nachteil der Historie für das Leben. Stuttgart 1998.
Jenseits von Gut und Böse. Berlin 1999.
Sämtliche Werke. Berlin 1999.
Werke. Berlin 2000.

Novalis (Hardenberg Friedrich Leopold von)

* 1772 Oberwiederstadt † 1801 Weissenfels

"Blood will flow through Europe until the nations come to understand the horrific madness that hounds them in a circle, until - struck by the holy music of reconciliation - they come to the altars of the past in a colourful blend to create a work of peace. ... Only faith can wake up Europe, make nations safe, and install Christianity in a new beauty visible around the world, in its ancient peacemaking office ...."

• German poet and prose writer, representative of Early Romanticism • influenced by his mother - a pietist • studies of philosophy and law at Jena, Leipzig, and Wittenberg Universities • disciple of F. Schiller and J. G. Fichte • friendship with the Schlegel brothers, founders of "The Jena Circle of Literature" • his work influenced by certain painful experiences - the deaths of his fiancée and his younger brother and his own serious illness •

Along with other members of the Romance-Germanic generation of the Romanticists, Novalis understood European issues in a passionate Catholic manner. He dreamed of a large European Council that would join all Christians and freethinkers, reformists, and mystics in a common "feast of love". He did not condemn the Protestants, but instead understood a lot of their motives and appreciated some of their conclusions, although he did not agree with their breaking away from the Church (he did not agree with their accusations as to the guilt of Catholicism or condemnation of the Pope). He called for a re-united, living, and effective Christianity (e. g. in his essay "Christianity or Europe"), with a Church which would not know state borders. In a united Europe, only the Church can ensure true freedom and bring about all the necessary reforms in a peaceful way. He was convinced that this vision would have to come true in the future, that Christianity would embrace all of Europe, make it united and blessed.

Die Christenheit oder Europa. Hamburg 1946.
Zázračná hra světa. Úvahy a fragmenty [Wonderful Play of the World. Considerations and Fragments]. Praha 1991.
Novalis Werke. München 2001.

ORTEGA Y GASSET JOSÉ

* 1883 Madrid   † 1955 Madrid

"Is it so certain that Europe is in decline, will abdicate the throne, and resign? Could this seeming decay actually be a healing crisis which will allow Europe to really be European? Europeans can only live if they have a great common goal in front of them. If this is missing, they will become plain and slack; their souls will crumble. The circles that we called nations for such a long time reached their widest extents a hundred years ago. Nothing more can be done with them, we can only overstep them. They are only the junk of the past, which is mounting both around and under a European, both oppressing and bothering him... . Only the decision to create one giant nation out of these national groups can revive Europe. Our continent should thus regain self-confidence and discipline, which would naturally induce great achievements from Europeans once again."

• Spanish philosopher, thinker, and writer • studies of philosophy and literature in Madrid and at German universities • influenced by neo-Kantism - later its critic • 1910-1916 Professor at Madrid University - founder of his own "Madrid school" of philosophy • 1914 founder of the "España" journal - author of political articles • from 1916 member of the Academy of Social and Political Sciences • from 1931 member of the Parliament and organizer of the Republican movement • 1936-1945 in exile - France, the Netherlands, Argentina, Portugal • 1946 founder of the Institute for Humanitarian Studies in Madrid • 1949-1951 great lecture tour around the U.S.A., Switzerland, and Germany •

His critical review of the state of Europe contained conclusions similar to Spengler's catastrophic visions, although Ortega's view of the future is not as hopeless. In his work "The Rebellion of the Masses" of 1930, he questioned the leading role of Europe in the world. He found Europe in a decline caused by nationalisms, which he labelled "the blind alleys of Europe", impulses acting against the creative powers of nations, the opposites of historical creative movements. He detested primitive national devices and the kind of people that employed them, especially as the "crowd nations" inevitably ended in the worst dictatorships.

He reached the conclusion that the role of Europe had been, and still was, irreplaceable and that total European decay would bring about a world in universal barbarism, spiritual impotence, and lack of morals. Therefore, after all his pessimistic findings, he expressed his conviction of the possibility of a European Renaissance, provided Europeans could find new great ideas and firm self-confidence and become strong, brave and tough once again.

The Revolt of the Masses. London 1951.
Úkol naší doby [Task of Our Days]. Praha 1969.
Europa y la idea de nación. Madrid 1985.
Europäische Kultur und europäische Völker. Stuttgart 1954.
Evropa a idea národa (a jiné eseje o problémech současného člověka) [Europe and the Idea of a Nation (and Other Essays on the Problems of Man of Our Days)]. Praha 1993.
Vzpoura davů [A Rebellion of the Masses]. Praha 1993.
La rebelión de las masas. Madrid 2000.

PALACKÝ FRANTIŠEK

* 1798 Hodslavice   † 1876 Prague

"*Nature does not contain any ruling or serving nations. If an alliance uniting several different nations into one political unit were firm and steady, no nation would have any reason to fear that this alliance would deprive them of any of their valuables; on the contrary, everyone would have a certain definite hope of protection by the central authority.*

... Being the youngest but not the weakest on the political scene of Europe, again, we have been moved to propose the summoning of a General European Congress of Nations to negotiate all international issues; we believe that free nations will be able to form resolutions more easily than paid diplomats. We hope that this proposal will be noticed before the reactionary policies of individual courts trigger malice and hate which will incite the nations to exterminate one another."

• Czech historian, philosopher, and politician • studies at evangelical schools in Trenčín and Bratislava • 1817-1823 private tutor to aristocratic families • 1823 arrival in Prague • archivist for the Šternberk family • 1831 national historiographer co-founder of the "Matice česká" (an institution for publishing scientific literature) • secretary of "The Royal Czech Society of Sciences" • founder and editor of "The Czech Museum Journal" • 1847 appointed to the Vienna Academy of Science • 1848-1849 deputy of the Constitutional Assembly - vision of a federal arrangement of the monarchy • 1848 Chairman of the Slavonic

Congress in Prague • leading representative of the Czech liberal policy • 1849-1861 departure from politics for scientific work • 1861-1872 deputy of the Czech Assembly • 1861 appointed to the "Upper House" of the Imperial Council • from 1863 passive resistance policy in the Imperial Council and in the Czech Assembly • 1865 revision of his previous approach to the monarchy in a series of eight articles - "The Idea of the State of Austria" • author of a monumental work "History of the Czech Nation in Bohemia and Moravia" •

Although there are many reasons justifying the use of Palacky's grand title "the father of the nation", it is not contradictory to speak about him in the context of Europeanism. Because of his desire to secure the existence of the small Czech nation, he was also forced to think in supranational dimensions. In this context, we have to understand that his frequently quoted statement about the Czech need for Austria, as well as its later, also frequently quoted correction, does not contradict his everlasting conviction that federalism is the best principle to ensure the liberty and the rights of all nations. In this sense, he conceived his proposal for the Imperial Constitution in 1848, and it is also the major theme of his "Ideas of the State of Austria". The federal re-arrangement of the Habsburg monarchy, wherein he found a lot of life-giving elements and links among the nations contained in it, could help establish a sound community for all the members of such a federation, protecting them against danger arising from Eastern Europe or from Asia. In particular he had in mind Russia, which was a living example of an unhappy universal monarchy. In his eyes, the Central European federalism of the Middle Ages was well matched to his vision of Pan-European federalism. He also appealed for solutions to the global problems of Europe to be sought - both as a spokesman of the Slavonic Congress and when quoting from its "Manifesto".

Idea státu Rakouského [The Idea of the State of Austria]. Praha 1907.
Palacký národu [Palacký to the Nation]. Praha 1898.
Františka Palackého korespondence a zápisky [František Palacký's Correspondence and Notes]. Praha 1902.

A History of the "Czechs" (also called "Bohemians") from their Origin, or rather
   from their First Known History. Seattle 1925.
Politická závěť [Political Testament]. Praha 1928.
Dílo [Works]. Praha 1941.
Politické projevy z let 1848-1864
   [Political Addresses from the Years 1848-1864]. Přerov 1947.
Österreichs Staatsidee. Wien 1972.
Úvahy a projevy [Considerations and Speeches]. Praha 1978.

PENN WILLIAM

* 1644 London   † 1718 Ruscombe

"The second objection is that the danger of effeminacy may come about if the trade of war is no longer practised... . Teach young people craftsmanship, natural philosophy, and diligence! This will make them neither females nor lions, but men, as the soldier is the very opposite of effeminacy. A knowledge of nature, however, along with the necessary and pleasant occupation of oneself with the arts, gives a man an understanding of himself and the world into which he was born, teaching him how he can become more helpful to others, how he can rescue and help in-

stead of wounding or destroying. It is also highly recommended to learn about the state of one's own homeland, about the state generally, and about individual European constitutions. This makes a man capable of functioning in Parliament, in the King's Council of their own country, in service at princely courts, or in a Confederacy of states."

• English religious reformer, Quaker • studies at Oxford • after forced expulsion from Oxford in 1666 custodian of the family estates in Ireland • 1668 imprisonment for publishing "The Sandy Foundation Shaken" • his most popular work "No Cross, no Crown" written in prison • 1671 arrested once again for his sermons • after his release, on a missionary journey to Germany and the Netherlands • 1681 receipt of a large territory in North America from the king (in recognizance of an inherited debt) • 1682 establishment of Pennsylvania - a colony for

persecuted co-religionists, with the most liberal Constitution of that time
• return to England • great influence at the court of James II •

He was a great pacifist and humanist (and had practical opportunities
for experimenting with his ideals in his Pennsylvania; Montesquieu called him a "modern Lycurgus"), presenting his ideas of European peace
and cooperation particularly in his proposal from 1692. His plan for
"The Association of Nations" is, in many aspects, similar to those of
previous thinkers. He theorized that European princes and kings, long-
ing for peace and order, would unite by establishing a common parliament
(imperial assembly), consisting of representatives from all European
countries (the number per country would depend on that country's annual income - Penn estimated a total of 90 deputies, including ten from
Russia and ten from Turkey). Where this parliament would meet was
not suggested. Great attention was devoted to procedural issues, e. g.
a round table, more doors leading to the assembly hall, the rotation of
chairmen, secret voting as a device against corruption, a three-quarters
majority (or at least a seven-vote absolute majority) necessary for passing a resolution, a method of storing documents, Latin or French as the
official languages, etc. This Parliament would have discussed the most
important European issues and resolved disputes among states when
there was a risk of war. It would have used military force against viola-
tors of peace. In such a community, free trade and travel would be
a matter of course. Like many of his followers, he also thought about
the possible consequences of the extinction of warfare, and he suggested a lot of new areas that Europeans might want to turn to. Like many
others, he believed that European rulers would show understanding for
a plan of general peace and prosperity, a well-established delusion that
reduced his proposal to nothing more than another entry in a long series
of utopias.

Völkerbundplan. Berlin 1920.
No Cross, no Crown. Boston 1947.
The Witness of William Penn. New York 1957.
Essai d'un projet pour rendre la paix de l'Europe solide et durable. York 1986.
An Essay towards the Present and Future Peace of Europe. London 1993.
The Peace of Europe. London 1993.

PETRARCA FRANCESCO (PETRARCH)

*1304 Arezzo † 1374 Arqua

"Take a look around; all of Gaul, the most remote part of our continent, and Britain, situated outside our continent, are weakened by oppressive wars. Germany, as well as Italy, suffers from internal conflicts and disputes, burning up in its own flame. Spanish kings are aiming their guns at one another .... . Greece cares only for itself.... . In other regions of Europe, Christ is either unknown or unwanted."

• famous Italian poet and scholar, founder of humanism • his father expelled from Florence along with Dante • 1313 follows his father to Avignon • studies in Montpellier, later at Bologna University • 1326 ordination at the lower stage • studies of the Ancient world • 1333 long study journey around France, Belgium, the Netherlands, and Germany, sponsored by the Colonne family • 1337 arrival in Rome • 1341 poetic coronation at the Capitol in Rome • from 1352 life in Italy - Milan, Venice, Padua • 1356 member of a delegation visiting Charles IV in Prague • author of biographies of famous Romans, poems, predominantly love poetry, "A Psalter", and "One Hundred Sonnets for Laura" •

Like Dante, Petrarch perceived European difficulties through his own bitter experiences in a divided Italy. Unlike Dante, he did not see an ideal model in the Roman Empire, but rather in the Roman Republic. With growing bitterness he observed Europe becoming involved in a growing number of military conflicts as new nations and nation states came into being. He also believed that the salvation of Europe could be found in

Christianity, even though the state the Catholic Church was in could not fill him with optimism. He was also unsuccessful in his search for a strong ruling personality who would put a stop to the disintegration of Italy as well as the whole of Europe. The hopes Petrarch had for Charles IV were also dashed, as Charles IV was aware of the unrealistic nature of such plans and rejected them. However, they continued to correspond.

Il Petrarca. Vinegia 1554.
Listy velkým i malým tohoto světa. Výbor z korespondence [Letters to the Great but also the Little of this World. Selection from Correspondence]. Praha 1974.
Die sechs Triumphe und die sechs Visionen des Herrn Francesco Petrarca. Leipzig 1988.

PICCOLOMINI AENEAS SILVIUS

* 1405 Corsignano   † 1464 Ancona

"Now (with the Turkish conquest of Byzantium - F. M.) we will be assaulted and killed in Europe itself, in our fatherland, in our home, in our dwelling place. ... Help us, Father, to gain victory over Your enemies, and when we finally regain Greece, we will sing hymns in Your name all over Europe."

• Italian humanist, diplomat, and historian • studies of law in Siena • life-long interest in Roman classical writers • 1432 supreme abbreviator of the council in Basel • from 1442 in Vienna; secretary to Frederick III, lectures on classical poetry at the local university • 1446 ordination • 1447 bishop in Trieste, Siena • 1451 member of the diplomatic delegation of Frederick III in Bohemia • 1456 Cardinal • 1458 Pope - Pius II •

Aeneas Silvius Piccolomini, as Pius II, the Pope in Rome, was an ardent opponent of the European plan of George of Poděbrady, even though he himself strove for European unity, under his own leadership. It was he who, for the first time in centuries, called on Europe as not only a geographical but also a historical and social entity. In the first two volumes of his large unfinished geographical work he tried to characterize and compare Europe with Asia, with his conclusions unambiguously favouring Europe. He saw his most important mission in the protection of Christianity against the Turks, either through persuasion or by violence. He identified Christianity with Europe (regarding non-

European Christians as a lower category). His appeals failed to find a significant response among European feudalists. On summoning European rulers to Ancona in 1464 (the same year as George of Poděbrady wanted to hold the first European Assembly) to organize a decisive crusade against the Turks, he found there only a few adventurers and persons of low repute. He died a few weeks after this fiasco.

Opera omnia. Basel 1571.
Historie česká [The Czech History]. Praha, date unknown.
Commentariorum Aeneae Sylvii Piccolominei Senensis. 1525.
Historia Bohemica. 1699.
Pojednání o vychování dítek [On Education of Children]. Praha 1906.
Epistula ad Mahumetem. Neapol 1953.
E. S. Piccolomini. Ausgewählte Texte aus seinen Schriften. Stuttgart 1960.

PROUDHON PIERRE JOSEPH

* 1809 Besançon   † 1865 Paris

"The federal system tames the disaffected feelings of the masses, as well as all ambitious and hate-mongering demagogues: it brings an end to the rule of the market; no soapbox orator will celebrate his triumph any more, nobody will wish to capture capital cities. ... Thus federation will be the salvation of the nation as it can protect it simultaneously against the tyranny of its own leaders and its own foolhardiness. ... After a revolution of ideas, the revolution of interests must necessarily come. The twentieth century will open the era of federations, in which mankind will emerge from a thousand-year purgatory once again."

• French politician and journalist • lyceum graduate • trained typographer, later owner of a printing house in Paris • 1840 essay "What is property?" • prosecuted for his opinions • 1846 work "Philosophy of Poverty" • 1848 elected to Parliament • 1849 founder of a people's bank offering interest-free credit • financial collapse • sentenced to prison • 1858-1862 exile in Brussels • 1863 return to Paris •

Proudhon was another great theoretician of federalism and perhaps even more vigorous than Rousseau, whom he studied closely, and the forefather of European democratic socialism. His key work "On The Federative Principle" was published only after his death.

He criticized centralized state systems built in a centralistic way, as well as unitarian great powers, as with them it was not possible to achieve a European balance and federalization. He did not believe that they could reach any further than to shaky coalitions as they would never give up even a part of their absolute sovereignty and were not able to compromise or at least partially subordinate themselves to common interests. In his opinion, the federal principle had an absolute moral priority over the unitarian system, which was subject to the unpredictability of unlimited and uncontrolled power.

He did not, however, believe that all of Europe could form one federative complex; instead he believed in a confederation of federations. As the first steps, he recommended the federalization of Italy, Greece, the Netherlands, Scandinavia, and the Danube countries. He regarded the decentralization of large states as the first stage of the disarmament process. Liberty for each nation was a necessary and essential precondition for all considerations and approaches leading to the unification of Europe.

De la justice dans la Révolution et dans l'Église. Tome 1.-3. Paris 1858.
Oeuvres complètes de P.-J. Proudhon. Paris 1959.
Du Principe Fédératif. Oeuvres complètes. Paris 1868.
De la capacité politique des classes ouvrières. Paris 1873.
Du principe de l'Art et de sa destination sociale. Paris 1875.
Über das föderative Prinzip und die Notwendigkeit, die Partei der Revolution wieder aufzubauen. Frankfurt a. M. 1989.
The Principle of Federation. Toronto 1991.
Selected Writings of Pierre-Joseph Proudhon. Garden City 1994.

RANKE LEOPOLD VON

* 1795 Wiehe † 1886 Berlin

"At present the life of man-kind is rooted in the nations of the Romance and Germanic tribes and in those of Slavonic and Hungarian origin who join-ed them and have assimilated with them. However varied our inner diversity, however diffe-rent and often hostile our ten-dencies, we still form a unity against other parts of the world. ... If we mention the Christian element, we do not understand by it solely religion, but neither the word culture nor civilization would express its meaning fully. It is the ge-nius of the West. It is the spirit which reshapes nations... ."

- German historian • studies of theology and philology at Leipzig University • 1818 grammar school teacher in Frankfurt an der Oder • 1825 invited to Berlin University as an associate Professor • 1836-1871 full professor of history in Berlin • from 1832 member of the Prussian Academy of Sciences • from 1841 official Prussian historiographer • 1854 member of the Prussian State Council • 1859 member of the commission for history of the Bavarian Academy of Sciences •

He is an anti-Hegelian, rejecting the mechanical application of dia-lectics. According to him, every nation gains the right to play a role in the history of the world only through its own culture. In his view, prio-rity was given to the European "Romance - Germanic" culture, in which Italy, France, and Spain represent one pole and Germany, England, and Scandinavia the other pole. Charlemagne formed Europe into one unit and under the leadership of the Pope and the Emperor of the Holy

Roman Empire the "unification of the whole of Europe" continued to strengthen. Ranke did not see a disaster for Europe in the subsequent fights between the Emperor and the Pope or between Catholicism and Protestantism, as this polarity was supposed to be part of the nature of things and the "European spirit could mature" through it.

Ranke considered the complex of Christian states of Europe as a whole connected by numerous relationships. He believed that strengthening state sovereignty was the most serious danger to European unity.

Historie de la papauté pendant les 16. et 17. siècles. Bruxelles 1844.
Deutsche Geschichte im Zeitalter der Reformation. Leipzig 1873.
Serbien und die Türkei im 19. Jahrhundert. Leipzig 1879.
Geschichte und Politik. Stuttgart 1940.
Völker und Staaten in der neueren Geschichte. Zürich 1945.
Über die Epochen der neueren Geschichte. Darmstadt 1980.
Historisch-politische Zeitschrift. Vaduz 1981.
Sämmtliche Werke. Leipzig 1986.
Die grossen Mächte. Frankfurt a. M. 1995.

RENAN JOSEPH ERNEST

* 1823 Trèguier   † 1892 Paris

"But what security could be equal to that Europe can offer now, when it re-confirms the present-day boundaries as embodied in old agreements and forbids anybody even to think of changing them? Any other solution would leave the gates and doors open for an infinite series of acts of revenge. If Europe makes this real, then fertile seeds will have been sown for a future central authority, in the manner of a Congress of the United States of Europe, which would guide the nations, put up resistance to them if necessary, and correct the national principle by a federative one."

• French philosopher, historian and philologist • educated in the seminary of Saint Nicolas near Paris • studies of theology - the lower degree of the priest's ordainment, later departure from the priesthood • from 1845 studies of history, philosophy, and Oriental studies • 1860 participant in an archaeological expedition to Syria • 1862 Professor at the department of Hebrew at the College de France • 1863 - his book "The Life of Christ" - a critical approach to Christ's divinity • stripped of his professorship after the scandal that followed • scientific expedition to Asia Minor and Greece • 1870 professorship restored • 1878 member of the French Academy •

He believed in progress and therefore saw the ideal of a unified Europe as a feasible one. But he realized - especially after his experience in the Franco-Prussian War in 1870 - how big an obstacle nationalism represented. He thought that the relations between the Germans and the French could only be resolved within the European framework. He stressed the fact that none of the European nations could be oppressed or weakened and that all of them must get rid of their "harmful dreams" - of expansion - by the mutual ratification of their boundaries. He rejected historical arguments for territorial claims, because nobody can say "where such archaeology would lead us to".

He rejected Herder's theory of a nation based on race, language, and the past and he contrasted it with the idea of a nation emerging from the consensus of its inhabitants to live together and of the fact that something great had been accomplished jointly and should continue in the future. Nations, for him, were nothing eternal - they came into existence and they will disappear again, maybe in a European confederation, which seemed to him to be a natural way out of the absurd conflicts inside Europe.

Filosofská dramata [Philosophical Dramas]. Praha 1890.
Život Ježíšův [The Life of Christ]. Praha 1896.
Apoštolové [Apostles]. Praha 1896, 1897.
Mélanges religieux et historiques. Paris 1904.
Vzpomínky z dětství a jinošství [Recollections from Childhood and Youth].
    Praha 1925.
Qu'est - ce qu'une nation? What is a nation? Toronto 1996.

Reynold Gonzaque de

* 1880 Cressier   † 1970 Fribourg

"The Germanic danger would never have arisen without the disunity and weakness of the Roman Empire. The Teutons were not numerous enough to conquer it. It is silly to speak about Germanic invasions... . Their political and social structures put the Teutons in contrast to the bureaucratic centralization of the Romans. Their constitution was federalist in the full sense of the word... - clans united into tribes, tribes united into a nation; a commonwealth of free people and warriors, the people's "thing", which survives in the country communities of the mountainous cantons in Switzerland

even nowadays. Hence the law which inserted mediators and dampers between both the extremes of the Roman law - the individual and the state - and so prevented the weaker part from being absorbed by the stronger. The idea of community really represents the principle of the Germanic law."

• Swiss literary and cultural historian, French-writing poet • renowned representative of Helvetian regionalism • author of papers on Swiss regions, their history, and legends • from 1915 Professor of French literature in Bern • from 1930 Professor at Freiburg University •

His eight-volume French-language work "The Foundation of Europe" has fundamental significance for Europeanism. For example, the reflections about the role of the Teutons are remarkable. He rejected the legends saying that the great incursions of the Teutons were the main cause of the fall of Rome. He appreciated the role of the Franks in the epoch following the fall of the Roman Empire, especially the personality of Charlemagne, the "Father of Europe". His opinion that the social conditions of the Teutons and their law form one of the main roots of European federalism is especially interesting. In the many disputes among historians, conducted frequently in the period between the two world wars, as to whether the past and the future of Europe are connected with Christianity or whether they are a result of the Renaissance, the Enlightenment, and the progress of science and technology, Reynold belongs in the camp of supporters of the first cultural and historical hypothesis.

L'Europe tragique. Paris 1934.
Die tragik Europas. Luzern 1935.
Intellectual Co-operation Organisation. Geneva 1938.
L'hellénisme et le génie européen. Fribourg 1944.
La formation de l'Europe. Paris 1953.
Europas Einheit: Jerusalem, Griechenland, Rom. München 1961.

ROMAINS JULES (FARIGOULE LOUIS)

* 1885 Saint-Julien-Chapteuil   † 1972 Paris

"Neither emperors nor kings, the less so the nations themselves, knew in fact why they had been so enthusiastic about making wars against one another and what they had wanted to reach through them. None of them thought of the charm of this continent, none of them thought of the even more fragile wonder of personal happiness in the world. This Europe of ours, the mother and educator of all nations and of every individual, the source of thoughts and inventions, the discoverer of the highest secrets, this Europe seemed less worthy for them than a flag, than a national anthem, a mother tongue, a country's boundary and a monument to military glory, less worthy than the cracking of phosphorus bombs and comparing the number of bombs dropped, less worthy than the satisfaction of the possible humiliation of neighbours."

• French poet, prose writer and dramatist • studies of philosophy at Paris University • 1909-1919 Professor of philosophy • literary activities • founder of unanimism • author of a twenty-seven-volume epic "The People of Good Will" • President of the PEN club • from 1946 member of the French Academy •

He belonged (along with R. Rolland) among the few great French personalities who raised their voices against the nationalistic madness that led to World War I, and even during the war he attempted to solve dissensions in a peaceful way and to unify Europe. That made him the victim of many a chauvinist attack.

ROMAINS JULES (FARIGOULE LOUIS)

He wished he did not have to warn Europe and mourn for it, but could praise it. He expressed these feelings in his poem "Europe" (1915) and in a number of collections of poetry and novels. He bravely supported the European system of defence in press campaigns. In the middle of the war he published a paper supporting Europeanism - "Pour que l'Europe soit", but his voice got lost in the atmosphere of nationalistic passions. Before World War II he initially supported the rights of Czechoslovakia, but unfortunately did not persist in that high-principled position.

Les hommes de bonne volonté. Paris 1933.
Lidé dobré vůle I.-IX. [People of Good Will]. Praha 1937-1938.

ROUGEMONT DENIS DE

* 1906 Neuchâtel   † 1985 Geneva

"Europe, which was started by bureaucracies, will become alive only with the help of the citizens who will live in it, who will be aware of their tasks with regard to this large whole that assures the liberties which are the basis of their civilization."

• Swiss by origin, philosopher and essayist writing in French • 1933 one of the founders of the personalistic movement in Paris • 1935-1936 university teacher at the University in Frankfurt am Main • 1941 professor at the Free School of Higher Learning in New York • 1966 founder and director of the European cultural centre in Geneva • 1953 and 1955 chairman of the round table of the Council of Europe • professor at the Institute of European studies in Geneva • corresponding member of the Academy of Ethical Studies and Politics in Paris • winner of many prizes and honorary doctorates •

De Rougemont was, without doubt, one of the most prolific writers ever to have addressed the problems of European integration. His writing contribution consists of dozens of commentaries, lectures, and evaluating reports. He showed his European spirit as early as 1946, when he returned to Europe from his WWII exile in the USA and gave his first address on the topic of the "European community". One year later he met Albert Einstein and together they discussed the integration of European nations. For instance, his contemplations from 1976-1977 about Europe and its regions, about moral responsibility in European economic cooperation, and about a Europe consisting of coalition states and federal nations, are very significant.

De Rougemont did not perceive the problems of European integration only on a political level, but he also interconnected them very closely with the ecological dimension. He did not limit himself merely to political problems connected with the European region, and he always perceived contemporary environmental problems in a global context. He felt a strong sense of common responsibility for the solution of the ecological crisis of the modern world. He articulated this in his book "Budoucnost je naše věc" [The future is in our hands] (which is one of his few works to be published in Czech). He never operated exclusively on a theoretical level - he was always willing to participate actively in practical matters (for instance at the conference "Europe and the Environment" in 1980 he fought for the preservation of Lake Geneva).

De Rougemont was also interested in the study of Europe in a cultural context. He presented his ideas at countless cultural conferences and in many organizations he was a member of. He is still the most important philosophical historian of European-ness. In 1970, he was deservedly awarded the European Prize of Robert Schuman.

Politique de la Personne.1934
Penser avec les Mains. 1936.
Liebe und das Abenland. 1939.
The Heart of Europe. New York 1941.
L'Europe en Jeu. Neuchâtel 1948.
L'Europe. Paris 1961.
Les Chances de l'Europe. 1962.
Europa. Vom Mythos zur Wirklichkeit. München 1962.
Lettre ouverte aux Européens. Paris 1970.
Du personnalisme au fédéralisme européen. Genève 1989.
Ecrits sur l'Europe. Paris 1994.
Budoucnost je naše věc [The future is in our hands]. Praha 1996.
The Idea of Europe. New York 1996.

ROUSSEAU JEAN-JACQUES

* 1712 Geneva   † 1778 Ermenonville

*"Never before that had a grea-
ter, more beautiful and more
useful plan than a proposal of
eternal and universal peace engaged the human mind. ... If
there is a way to solve dangerous antagonisms, then it can
only be done by a federal government which will unite nations with bonds similar to
those which connect individuals and which subdue both
nations and individual persons
to the authority of laws. Such
a government should be given
priority over all others as it
will have respect both for big
and small states... . Besides
these official unifications, some
others too, less prominent, but*

*nevertheless real, can be brought to life discreetly, through interest
groups, through passing principles, unifying habitual practice, or
through other means. All European powers should form a system
which will unite them by the same religion, law, manners, sciences,
trade, and by the balance which would necessarily result from it and
which would... not be as easy to break as many people believe."*

• French philosopher and writer • 1728 departure from Geneva to
France • various occupations, short stay in the seminary, wandering
about Switzerland and France • 1741 return to Paris acquaintanceship
with Diderot and Grimm • 1743 secretary at the Embassy in Venice •
return to Paris after disagreement with the Ambassador - the first important papers • collaboration on the "Encyclopaedia" (especially articles
on music) • from 1761 stay at the estate of his patron Marshal de

Luxembourg in Montmorency • 1761-1762 works "A Social Contract" and a book on pedagogy "Émile, or On Education" (the deistic chapter "The Confession of Faith of a Savoy Vicar" became a source of indignation, the work was condemned to be burnt by a court decision, and a warrant for the author's arrest was made out) • 1762-1767 travels around Switzerland, Prussia, and England • quarrels with friends • 1767 return to France • serious mental illness at the end of his life •

He considered himself the inventor of the system of federalism, the principles of which he perhaps wanted to elaborate in a subsequent part of the book "A Social Contract" (it is unclear whether it was stolen, damaged, or not written at all). But he spoke about the principles in his "Considerations on the Government of Poland", written at the request of Polish conspirators. They asked him to elaborate a constitution for their country which could prevent its tragic division. The essence of his recommendations consists in the radical federalization of Poland on the basis of the existence of free communities with as much liberty as possible. He thinks that national education is not a menace but a basic condition for such a republican federation. As for the unification of Europe, he expressed his opinion in the "Extract from the Project of Eternal Peace of the Abbé of Saint-Pierre". This discourse was written to order and published in Amsterdam in 1761. (The ideas of Saint-Pierre were widely spread only through being published in this form). The "Judgement of the Eternal Peace", containing more critical reservations, was published only after his death. Rousseau rejected the role of sovereigns and of their European Congress or federation, and put the unification of Europe directly into the hands of nations.

Extrait du projet de paix perpetuelle de M. l'Abbé de Saint-Pierre. Amsterdam 1761.
Jugement sur la paix perpétuelle. Genf 1782.
Considérations sur le Gouvernement de Pologne. Oeuvres complètes VII. Paris 1857.
Zum ewigen Frieden. Berlin 1920.
O původu nerovnosti mezi lidmi [On the Reason for Inequality among People]. Praha 1949.

O společenské smlouvě neboli o zásadách státního práva [On a Social Contract or on the Principles of the State Law]. Praha 1949.

Rozpravy [Debates]. Praha 1978.

Kulturkritische und politische Schriften. Berlin 1989.

Saint-Pierre Charles Irénée Castel de

* 1658 Saint-Pierre-Église   † 1743 Paris

"I had to start with the idea that European rulers, just like all other people, need peace, and that they would be happier in one alliance of nations ... I do not think that the forming of a united Europe would be more complicated than was the forming of the German Empire in the past; it is just a question of repeating something that was achieved in the past, only on a bigger scale now."

• French journalist, philosopher, and reformer • one of the first pioneers of the French Enlightenment and of ideas of humanism • significant philanthropist and advocate of social solidarity • member of many literary salons • 1694 member of the French Academy • 1712 participant in peace talks in Utrecht - together with Cardinal de Polignac • 1713 release of the "Project of Eternal Peace" •

The Abbé de Saint-Pierre grew up in a family country mansion and he received higher education only at grammar school. He was said to be neither a talented writer nor to have a noble spirit, but the good that he did for his fellow-citizens and for the public made him a genius. He is said to have been an eloquent orator, which is documented by the fact that he was awarded a prize for eloquence. His linguistic works are also highly valued. This French social philosopher was an advocate of natural religions and he admired the economic theories of the physiocrats. His thoughts comprise a set of utilitarian and philanthropic motives. He believed that the state should establish a just taxation system, including graduated income tax, and that state services should even include free public education both for men and women. The state should further guarantee improved transportation to promote, above all, the development of trade. He supported the abolition of aristocratic privileges and the decentralization of administration. In his "Discourse on Polysynody" he proclaimed the ideals of a constitutional monarchy, which should be based on the pillars of advisory organs and an academy of experts. In this paper he also criticized the government of Louis XIV, which led to his expulsion from the Academy.

One of his pro-European works stands out above the rest - "Project de paix perpetuelle" (Project of Eternal Peace) - which he first wrote when the peace treaty of Utrecht was signed in 1713. He informed the general public about this project a year later. In the project, he presented his innovative ideas envisaging a European organization which should guarantee the peaceful coexistence of European nations. It was a plan for an international court and a league of nations. This European "Union of Nations" was not supposed to meddle in the internal affairs of individual states, and their rulers would not be allowed to trade territories or conclude treaties without the approval of a $3/4$ majority of its members. Commercial laws should be the same for all nations. It would not be possible to wage war against a country which had not been previously declared an enemy of the whole "Union of Nations". Everything was supposed to be decided by the Union Council. In spite of some interesting ideas proposed by the Abbé de Saint-Pierre in his peace plan, his project fell into oblivion without much response. But in the course of time it inspired many other European thinkers (Voltaire, Montesquieu), and became popular especially because of the interest of Rousseau, who published de Saint-Pierre's ideas and commented on and developed them in his own reflections.

Project de paix perpetuelle. Paris 1713.

Saint-Simon Claude Henri Rouvroy de

* 1760 Paris   † 1825 Paris

"Undoubtedly the time will come when all the nations of Europe will recognize that the problems concerning every single person will have to be solved before they start to be interested in dealing with the problems of nations as such. Then all nuisance will be less obvious, disturbances will be laid to rest, wars will cease to exist. That is the target we are aimed at all the time, such is the human spirit that bears us up to such heights! But who deserves human wisdom more, he who drags his heels on his way to it or he who hurries to find it as soon as possible?"

• French philosopher and economist, social utopian • 1779 participant in the War of Independence in the United States • 1782 officer of French troops in Lorraine • 1783 departure from the army for financial reasons • 1787 journey to Spain • 1789 return to France • participant in the Revolution • 1794 arrested and kept in prison due to the "Ordinance on Suspects" • 1795 successful entrepreneur • 1805 loss of his property, entirely dependent on occasional earnings and financial support of his valet • 1814 a treatise "On the Reorganization of European Society" •

After Napoleon's fall he wrote, together with his secretary A. Thierry, a treatise on the reorganization of Europe, in which he suggested the establishment of a "Union of European Nations", which should protect Europe from economic and political disruption and further wars. A rapprochement of the French with the English, as well as with the

SAINT-SIMON CLAUDE HENRI ROUVROY DE

unified Germans, would serve as its basis. Saint-Simon laid particular emphasis on the economic aspects of the unification and it might be possible to say that it was thanks to his ideas that the Montane Union and the Common Market came into existence in the middle of the 20th century.

His principle of a union of nations is federalistic. Every nation should have its own parliament, which would recognize the sovereignty of the general parliament, which would arise from general points of view and needs - from "European patriotism". Representatives of four "corporations" - businessmen, scientists, clerks, and administrators - would enter the European parliament by direct election; every million literate Europeans would send one congressman of each category for a period of ten years (assuming 60 million voters, it would mean about 240 congressmen). The European Parliament should have power over, and property rights in, the region and the city where it would be situated. It would provide funding, as necessary, to all the members of the Federation and it would run major European projects (a real project was given: the Danube-Rhine-Baltic Sea Canal). Saint-Simon could see the best way of ensuring general peace in the fact that nations would be busy with these great projects. All the Earth was to be populated by the European race, as it is the best one and would be able to raise all mankind to its level.

The European Parliament was also to be responsible for education, ensuring freedom of conscience and worship, and for the development of a moral code and for suppressing everything that would work against its spirit.

Saint-Simon's plan interrupted a long line of projects of European princely alliances by virtue of the fact that it was based on the democratic principle of the will of the nations themselves, expressed by their elected representatives.

New Christianity. London 1834.
Výbor z díla [Selected Works]. Praha 1950.
Selected Writings. New York 1952.
De la réorganisation de la Societé européenne. Lausanne 1967.
Slova [Words]. Praha 1992.

Schelling Friedrich Wilhelm Joseph von

* 1775 Leonberg   † 1854 Bad Ragaz

"Whatever the ultimate aim, it is clear that the right unity can be reached only through religion. Not that the state would control the religion or the religion the state, but the state in itself should develop the religious principle; a large union of nations should rest on the basis of a religious conviction which would become general."

• German philosopher, Fichte's disciple, Goethe's friend, Hegel's opponent • 1790-1795 studies of theology, philology, and philosophy in Tübingen • 1794 first philosophical treatise • 1797 his work "Thoughts on Natural Philosophy" • 1798 Professor at Jena University • from 1803 Professor in Würzburg - harbinger of "the philosophy of identity" • 1841 called to Berlin as counterbalance to Hegelian radicalism, but unsuccessful in pushing forward his irrationalist doctrine •

A circle of thought represented by Herder, Kant, and Novalis closes with him. (Schelling is similar to the last-mentioned also in his conversion to Catholicism.) He became one of the most influential propagators of the idea of Europeanism in the 19th century. He influenced both his Romantic contemporaries and later thinkers (e. g. Schopenhauer, Bergson, the "Slavophiles" et al.).

In the idea of a community of states and in the international law court he saw the coronation of "the epoch of nature", or rather its crowning event, which follows the "epoch of fate" and announces "the epoch of providence". He presumed that no matter how unsuccessful the attempt to create European unity by means of the church was (since the church took on the elements and forms of a state instead of remaining pure, untouched by anything coming from outside), the religious way - after the failure of the attempts of states - nevertheless seemed to be the only hopeful one.

Výbor z díla [Selected Works]. Praha 1977.
System des transzendentalen Idealismus. Leipzig 1979.
Filosofická zkoumání bytnosti lidské svobody a s tím souvisejících předmětů. Komentáře. [Philosophical Research into the Existence of Human Freedom and Issues Relating to it. Annotations.] Praha 1992.
Ausgewählte Schriften. Frankfurt a. M. 1995.
Philosophische Untersuchungen über das Wesen der menschlichen Freiheit und die damit zusammenhängenden Gegenstände. Hamburg 1997.
The Ages of the World. Albany 2000.
Briefe. Stuttgart 2001.

Schiller Johann Christoph Friedrich von

* 1759 Marbach   † 1805 Weimar

"Be embrac'd, ye millions yonder!
Take this kiss throughout
*   the world!*
Brothers--o'er the stars unfurl'd
Must reside a loving Father.
...

As the suns are flying, happy
Through the heaven's glorious
*   plane,*
Travel, brothers, down your lane,
Joyful as in hero's vict'ry.
...

Suffer on courageous millions!
Suffer for a better world!
O'er the tent of stars unfurl'd
God rewards you
*   from the heavens."*

("Ode to Joy",
Translated by William F. Wertz)

• German dramatist, poet and art theorist • representative of literary Classicism • 1773 Military Academy in Ludwigsburg by order of the Duke of Württemberg - personal experience of tyranny • adherent of the "Sturm und Drang" Movement • studies of law and medicine in Stuttgart • 1780 regimental doctor • 1782 first night of "the Robbers" in Mannheim, thunderous applause from young people - a split with the Duke followed, Schiller was arrested and forbidden to write • 1783 leaving for Mannheim - dramatic and poetic works • editor of "Rheinische Thalia" magazine • 1788 post of Professor of history at Jena University at Goethe's intercession • from 1794 friendship and collaboration with Goethe • 1802 elevated to the peerage •

Like Lessing, Herder, and Kant, Schiller too was under the influence of Rousseau and thanks to him he got acquainted with the Abbé de Saint-Pierre's plan. He was brought into ecstasy by the hopes raised by the Great French Revolution. The revolutionary Convention called him "a poet - a friend of mankind" and he was even appointed a freeman of the French Republic. However, he did not share Cloots' illusions of the Neo-Roman - French revolutionary melting of Europe; his idea was a federalistic one. He saw the best basis of the European community in supranational unions coming out of the Reformation (here he was completely different from e. g. Schlegel or Novalis). He was one of the first to accentuate the fact that there had been a unity of morals and customs and uniformity of institutions as early as in medieval Europe. In general, he stressed the role which Europe has played in the history of mankind. (It is typical that his and Beethoven's "Ode to Joy" has become an artistic symbol of the European Union and the Council of Europe.)

Nesmrtelná slova [Immortal Words]. Praha 1940.
J. W. Goethe. Briefwechsel mit Friedrich Schiller. Zürich 1950.
Geschichte des Dreissigjährigen Krieges. München 1958.
Universalhistorische Übersicht. München 1958.
Óda na radost [Ode to Joy]. Praha 1980.
Výbor z filozofických spisů [Selected Philosophical Works]. Praha 1992.
Was heisst und zu welchem Ende studiert man Universalgeschichte? Jena 1996.
Schillers Werke. Weimar 2001.
Gedichte. Ditzingen 1999.

SCHLEGEL KARL WILHELM FRIEDRICH VON

* 1772 Hanover   † 1829 Dresden

"And it is nothing but the variety of differences that makes Europe what it is, what gives it perfection, the merit of being a remarkable seat of the life and education of mankind. If only one Rome existed, in which everything were to merge and pass away, instead of a free and rich Europe, we would be offered a period of sad monotony of Chinese chronicles through the annals of one Roman Empire instead of the rich history of Europe... ."

• German literary critic, poet • studies of law at Göttingen University, afterwards classical languages in Leipzig • 1794-1802 stays in Dresden, Jena, and Berlin in turn • studies of oriental languages and Sanskrit in Paris • after 1808 in the Austrian civil service; participant in the Congress of Vienna • co-founder of the literary "Jena Circle" of the Romanticists • co-publisher of the "Athenäum" magazine •

A founder of the first European magazine - "Europe" - published in Frankfurt am Main and run from Paris (in the years 1803-1805). This convert to Catholicism presented in it his own Romantic ideals as well as those of his associates (Novalis, Görres, Schelling, Baader et al.), according to whom Europe was created and could be preserved only by Christianity. In the Christian history of Europe he saw the hope for the future of the continent. He considered the Empire of Charlemagne and the famous period of the papacy the apogee of the history of Europe; he also admired Charles V as a hero and "the warrior of the century", one of the last supporters of European unity; after him there came a decline which had not even reached its nadir in the 19th century. But he did not despair of Europe, which he could see as the setting of a historic struggle between good and evil, in which the fate of all mankind would be decided. Along with Hegel, he could see the ultimate destiny of history in Europe. Besides the virtue of unity, he also recognized the merits of diversity to a much greater extent than his contemporaries.

Vorlesungen über die neuere Geschichte. Wien 1846.
Vorlesungen über Karl V. Wien 1846.
Philosophical Fragments. Minneapolis 1991.
Fragmente zur Geschichte und Politik. Zürich 1995.
Vorlesungen und Fragmente zur Literatur. München 2002.

SCHMID CARLO

* 1896 Perpignan   † 1979 Bonn

"Which qualities are characteristic for a man of Europe? This is an endlessly complex issue, and moreover it is a question which can be answered in a dangerously high and disturbing number of ways.

In spite of that, I would like to look for some signs that could at least bring nearer the beginning of some answers for us. I do believe that there are some that are able to suggest which direction we should search in. But it can happen that the answer we will find will be nothing but the shadow play Plato spoke about: a play of shadows which are the essence of things cast on the walls of a cave to which we are chained."

• German politician • studies of law • 1927-1940 a judge from 1945 member of the Social Democratic Party of Germany (in German SPD) • 1946-1953 Professor of international law at Tübingen University • 1953-1968 Professor of political science in Frankfurt am Main • 1947 to 1973 member of the presidium of the SPD • 1948-1949 member of the German parliamentary council • 1949-1953 congressman of the Federal Assembly for the SPD • 1966-1969 federal minister for the affairs of the federal lands • 1969-1972 Vice-President of the Federal Assembly •

Particularly in his paper "On the Man of Europe", he tried to cover at least some of the characteristic aspects of the people of Europe.

They are: liberalism, the ability to oppose fate or despotism; rejection of a quiescent existence, and, on the other hand, permanent efforts to be a discoverer, creator, and master of nature; bearer of the weight of history, simultaneously endeavouring to understand it as well as to cast off its yoke when they can see a better perspective; experiencing collective consciousness and conscience but overcoming them by achieving individual consciousness and conscience; asking for the respect of society for individual reason, conscience and dignity, but also demanding the same things from individuals in relation to other individuals and other communities; searching for truth and the development of science, philosophy, and arts originating in it, and recognizing liberty, equality, and the law as the bases of human society. In such features Schmid could see the contribution of a European to all of mankind. But he himself did not consider his characteristics either complete or impossible to discuss.

Deutschland und der europäische Rat. Köln 1949.
Über den europäischen Menschen. In: Die Neue Rundschau 1950.
Tätiger Geist. Hannover 1964.
Essays zur Literatur und Politik. Tübingen 2001.

SCHUMAN ROBERT

* 1886 Luxembourg   † 1963 Scy-Chazelles

"To have real peace everywhere, we first need a unified Europe. ... Europe will not be built overnight or after a universal general plan. It will be built according to concrete results which will first create solidarity de facto. ... Common regulations of coal and steel production will lead directly to the creation of a common basis for economic development as the first step towards European integration."

• French politician and statesman • studies of law at Bonn, Munich, and Berlin Universities • from 1912 prosecuting counsel at the German court in Metz • 1919-1940 deputy in the French Parliament 1940 Secretary of State for the affairs of refugees • disagreements with Petain and the occupation authorities • arrested and deported to Germany • 1942 escape and entry into the French resistance movement • 1945 co-founder of the French Republican Party of the People • 1946-1947 Minister of Finance • 1947-1948 Prime Minister • 1949-1952 Minister of Foreign Affairs • 1955-1958 Minister of Justice • 1958-1960 Chairman of the European Parliament • 1960-1963 Honorary Chairman of the European Parliament •

Along with J. Monnet, he contributed to the about-turn in the relation of France towards European unity. Unlike de Gaulle's conception of a union of sovereign states, he tried to see through, in the spirit of integration, the creation of unity in all the spheres of life of the nations who would decide to establish an association. Schuman's proposal to create a Montane Union or a European Coal and Steel Community originated in 1950 (in collaboration with Monnet again) from his consideration of the Allies' methods of administering the natural resources of defeated Germany and afterwards from involving its western part - the German Federal Republic - in the economy of democratic Europe. His public proclamation of such an intention on May 9, 1950 is considered the symbolic start of the integration process.

His plan was accepted in the following year at the Paris conference of six western European countries - Belgium, France, Italy, Luxembourg, the Netherlands, and the German Federal Republic (in which Chancellor Konrad Adenauer supported the tendencies to join the western European economy, especially after the reconciliation of Germany with France). In 1952 he worked out a project for a European Union of Defence. He accomplished his European activities in the office of the Chairman of the European Parliament in Strasbourg. From those projects the way led towards European communities and the present-day European Union. R. Schuman was given by history the opportunity to take part in the first real steps which started the fulfilment of the dream of European unity that had been envisioned for centuries. On 9th May Europeans commemorate the birthday of United Europe (popularly known as "St. Schuman's Day").

Pour l'Europe. Paris 2000.

Spaak Paul Henri

* 1899 Schaerbeek   † 1972 Brussels

"It is necessary to build up Europe. It is necessary to start building it up now, if Europe wants to build itself up into a dignified continent. ... I never supported the opinion that European society should be a community of the Six - closed, autarchic, self-concerned, egoistic, ... insensitive to the problems which we have created for others by signing the Treaty of Rome. If we withdraw into our shell, ... we shall be destroyed."

• Belgian diplomat and statesman • studies of law in Brussels • soldier in WWI, POW in Germany for 2 years • member of the Belgian Socialist Party • 1935-1936 Minister of Transport • 1936-1939 and 1940 Minister of Foreign Affairs • 1938-1939 Prime Minister • 1940 exile - minister of the government in exile in London • 1946 president of the General Assembly of the United Nations • 1947-1949 Prime Minister • 1944-1949, 1954-1957, 1961-1966 Minister of Foreign Affairs • 1946 chairman of the General Assembly of the United Nations • 1957-1961 Secretary General of NATO • president of the Royal Belgian Academy of French Language and Literature • co-founder of Benelux •

Spaak was one of the most outstanding personalities in post-war Europe, one of the main architects of the European Economic Community, and a categorical advocate of an economically and politically united Europe. During his long political career he fulfilled an incredible number of leading functions in European organizations and he was many a time a member of Belgian governments. One of the specific features of his political life was that if he could not enforce his ideas and policy, he would resign from his functions. He was a gifted negotiator and speaker. In exile in Britain during WWII, he met Jean Monnet and Winston Churchill, who became his role model. As early as when he was in his London exile, Spaak contemplated the future arrangement of Europe. It was clear to him that there must be a common organization of European states. The aim was a united Europe. The first model of such an organization was Benelux, the formation of which he initiated (in 1944, a customs union treaty was signed by Belgium, the Netherlands, and Luxembourg).

After the war, Spaak enjoyed international popularity as the Secretary-General of the United Nations. A little later - in 1948 - he was one of the initiators of the Treaty of Brussels and the Organization for European Economic Cooperation (OECE, the predecessor of today's OECD). Spaak was the chairman of the council of this organization, whose aim was to distribute American aid within the framework of the Marshall Plan. He perfectly understood that this Plan could be used to compel the European countries to cooperate. After the European Congress in the Hague in 1948 he was elected the chairman of the Parliamentary Assembly of the Council of Europe, which was to become the European Parliament (according to the original intentions). However, the Council of Europe did not live up to his expectations and Spaak continued to focus on economic cooperation, which, according to him, if complemented by political will, could lead to the unification of Europe and thus to the heading off of all potential military conflicts on the European continent.

He concentrated on the newly-formed European Coal and Steel Community, and he became the chairman of the Parliamentary Assembly of this organization. The second projected organization, the European Defence Community, ultimately failed to come into existence as the treaty was not ratified by the French Parliament. Nevertheless, Spaak did not give up and he initiated negotiations about the establishment of a customs and economic union. He became the head of a committee of government representatives and experts from Benelux, Italy, and Germany (the so-called "Spaak committee"). At the end of their negotiations, Spaak's report was adopted, which became in 1957 the basis for the Treaties of Rome, which laid the foundations of the European Communities.

The last stop in his international political life was as the Secretary-General of NATO. He resigned from this function after failing to settle disputes between the USA and France, which was represented by General de Gaulle. Spaak left the world of top-level politics in 1966, when he voted in the Belgian Parliament (against his party) for the motion that the NATO headquarters should move to Belgium. After this, he resigned from his Parliamentary seat. For his unflagging effort to create a politically and economically united Europe, he was awarded the Charlemagne Prize in Aachen in 1957.

A New Effort to Build Europe. Foreign Affairs, Vol. 43, No. 2, 1965.
Memoiren eines Europäers. Hamburg 1969.

SPENGLER OSWALD

* 1880 Blankenburg   † 1936 Munich

"A *culture is born at the moment of a great soul's awakening from a primal state of
mind... . A culture dies when
the soul has exhausted all its
possibilities. That is the reason
for all ends in history (cultures
have to grow both internally
and externally until they reach
the point at which they culminate and then die), from which
the end of Classical times can
be seen in front of you in the
brightest colours, whereas these
days we can already feel in
ourselves the earliest traces of
our own, quite similar event as
far as its course and duration
are concerned; an event which*
belongs to the first centuries of the next millennium, which is the
decline of the West!"

• German philosopher and historian • studies of philosophy and
mathematics at Halle, Munich, and Berlin Universities • grammar school
teacher of philosophy in Hamburg, from 1911 in Munich • 1918-1920
his fundamental work on philosophy of history "The Decline of the
West" • representative of the theory of historical cycles • adherent of
monarchism, traditionalism, and Prussian militarism • 1933 refusal to
cooperate with Hitler and Nazism • boycotted till his death •

Better than almost anybody else, he was able to analyse the state
of a Europe filled with controversies which resulted in wars. He was
afraid of the fatal consequences which could be brought about by the
steadily growing tendencies of our continent to decay. On the basis of
his research of Europe past and present, he reached the conclusion of

a cyclic process of the birth, rise, and decay of cultures and civilizations (by which he also developed Hegel's and Toynbee's thoughts). On them, he based his reasoning for his very pessimistic vision of Europe. He foretold an impending era of Caesarism, a callous power growing out of blood and the desire to dominate, which Hitler, in no time, confirmed through his dictatorship in Germany.

He adopted Nietzsche's way of facing a catastrophe and being able to reconcile fate with one's own destiny but he also stuck to the Faustian myth of an active and creative human individuality. The thoughts in his work "The Decline of the West" point to the causes of European catastrophes (World War I was just the first act) and they foretell the end of Europe - frighteningly similar to that of Rome in its fate.

Pessimismus? Berlin 1922.
Reden und Aufsätze. München 1937.
The Decline of the West. New York 1999.
Der Untergang des Abendlandes. Umrisse einer Morphologie der Weltgeschichte. München 2000.
Le Déclin de l'Occident. Paris 2000.

STAËL-HOLSTEIN ANNE LOUISE GERMAINE DE

* 1766 Paris   † 1817 Paris

"In our modern days we need a European spirit... . The human mind consists of two very different powers: one that creates in us the need to accept facts trustingly and the other that orders us to review and investigate. Neither of these abilities must be satisfied on account of the other: Protestantism and Catholicism owe thanks for their rise not to Luther or the Popes; this way of thinking would mean our observing history in a very wrong way, if we attributed their development to such a chain of coincidences. Protestantism and Catholicism live in the hearts of people."

• French writer, literary critic, essayist • daughter of the Minister J. Necker • interest in politics from youth • 1781 first literary reflections • 1789 affection for the ideas of the Great French Revolution • 1792 criticism of violence and terror in France • 1793 journey to England • 1795-1803 Paris - her salon a place of meetings and debates of liberal society - philosophers and media people • initially an admirer of Napoleon, later a critic • 1803 expelled from Paris • travels about Europe - Italy, Russia, Switzerland • meets J. W. Goethe and F. Schiller in Weimar • after Napoleon's defeat return to France •

She was the very opposite of a contemporary of hers (and at a time also a neighbour) - Joseph de Maistre - conciliatory, prompting to ecumenicity and federalism (in relations among nations). She did recognize a hope for Europe in what once created and unified it - Christianity, but she did not see war and the destruction of everything non-Catholic as a means of overcoming the schism, but compromise, understanding, and raising the spirit of Europeanism. Her salon was a practical example of realizing such a way. She especially promulgated the role of literature as a means for the mutual enrichment of nations and understanding among them and she encouraged translation, since even a nation with excellent literature remains poor if it does not know the literary fruits of other nations. She put the exchange of thoughts in the first place in the process of the unification of Europe.

Lettres sur les ouvrages et le caractère de J. J. Rousseau, Paris 1788.
Oeuvres complètes. Paris 1820.
De l'Allemagne. Paris 1878.
Memoiren. Berlin 1912.
Politics, Literature, and National Character. London 2000.
De la littérature considérée dans ses rapports avec les institutions sociales.
    Paris 1860.

SULLY BÉTHUNE MAXIMILIEN DE

* 1560 Rosny-sur-Seine   † 1641 Villebon

"First I presented to the King (of England - F. M.) a general conception of the project of unification of all the states to which the curbing of the power of the House of Austria had to be a matter of concern, and where the union of France, England, and the Netherlands would form the basis for defence as well as aggression, strengthened by the closest links between the Bourbons and the Stuarts. I let him know at first sight that this kind of connection would be easy to accomplish. From the side of Denmark and Sweden, in short of all the Protestant Dukes, there would not be any problems. It might also be possible to make it positive for the Catholic masters..., German Dukes (if everything that the Austrian House in Germany possessed could be distributed among them), Austria, the Hungarian Lands, Moravia, Silesia, etc. (the old rights would be given back to them), for the Pope himself, if he were granted full ownership of all the countries which he had had only in fief up to those days."

• French statesman and commander • minister of Henry IV of Navarre • came from an Huguenot family • 1593 conversion to Catholicism • from 1596 member of the Royal Board (finances) • 1597-1609 author of the reorganisation of the tax system, national debt redeemed • 1599 grand master of artillery • state supervisor of the construction of waterways and other means of communication • support for agriculture, silk production, and trade • 1602 Governor of the Bastille • 1604 Governor in Poitou • from 1606 Duke and French peer • forced to resign his office after the death of Henry • 1634 Marshal •

His "great plan" is not a compact document; it consists of individual parts spread over the 1000 pages of his "Memoires" (the whole title takes about 6 lines), the first volumes of which date from the year 1638. In them, he reflects on his long and eventful life, which leads him on to consider European questions in a predominantly French nationalist and strong anti-Austrian tone (as an ambassador of the French king he tried to make - expressed in a more modern terminology - "a London - Paris axis"), up to a supranational attitude. Sully's European project took into account five electing monarchies (he included the Holy Roman Empire of the German nation, the Papal State, the Czech Lands, Poland, and Hungary in it), six hereditary kingdoms (England, Denmark, France, Lombardy, Spain, and Sweden) and four republics (Belgium, Venice, Italy, and Switzerland) into a European Union ("a Christian Republic of Europe"). Such a confederation would be governed by six provincial councils (e. g. in Vienna there would be the seat of a provincial council for eastern Europe) and a central "General Council" (whose headquarters was to rotate around the cities of central Europe), whose decisions would be obligatory for all states. All nations, and all religions, too, would be equal. Nevertheless, for the states situated on the borderline with the enemies of Europe, the Union would play a role in which, on the one hand, it would take over the duties of defence, but, on the other, the eight most influential sovereigns of the Union would have the right to elect their rulers (it would have concerned Poland, the Hungarian Lands, and the Czech Lands - the plan considered re-establishing their independence). Free trade based on removing customs borders should bring together a politically united Europe in the economic field too, so that internal wars could be discounted for once and for all. This sounded very noble in a Europe tossed about by the Thirty Years' War, but those who should have been affected by Sully's ideas failed to appreciate them and so their father finished his days in complete seclusion far from the corridors of power.

Mémoires de Maximilien de Béthune, duc de Sully, principle ministre de Henry le Grand. Londres 1745.

Denkwürdigkeiten Maximilian von Béthune, Herzogs von Sully. Zürich 1786.

Sully's Grand Design of Henry IV. From the Memoirs of Maximilien de Béthune, duc de Sully (1599-1641). London 1931.

TOYNBEE ARNOLD JOSEPH

* 1889 London   † 1975 London

"We, Western people, endorse, just because we are people, the belief that what we have done to the world in recent centuries is unparalleled. There exists an efficacious remedy for this Western illusion. It is only necessary to look back to what the Greeks and the Romans did to the world not so long ago and we will arrive at it: they too, attacked the world in their day; they too, believed for a long time as if they were different from other people... . Of course, I do not intend to say by this that we can set a horoscope for our own future by studying what happened ... in Greek-Roman history and simply by mechanically applying these events to the modern West. ... If we gaze into the future, we fumble in the dark and we have to avoid believing that we can mark clearly the hidden way lying ahead of us. And yet we would be fools not to make full use of any ray of light which greeted our eyes... ."

• English historian, philosopher, and sociologist • during WWI in diplomatic service • 1919 participant in the Paris Peace Conference • 1919-1924 Professor of history and Greek at Oxford University • 1925-1955 Director of the Royal Institute of International Affairs in London • author of a ten-volume work "A Study of History" • at the time of WWII in diplomatic service again • 1946 member of delegation to peace negotiations in Paris • adherent of the theory of four stages of civilization: birth, rise, decline, and decay •

TOYNBEE ARNOLD JOSEPH

His comparative historic work "The World and the West" introduced somewhat unconventional opinions on Europe and its role in the world. He listed a balance of major crimes - seen through the eyes of non-Europeans - which our continent committed against the other continents, and so his conclusions are in fact accusations. Especially in the period from the 15th century till the year 1945 the West could mostly be found in the position of an aggressor. He refused to acknowledge the civilizing pride of the Europeans who, even though they admitted oppressing the conquered countries, defended their actions through the unparalleled contribution of civilization. He found analogies between Greek and Roman conquests of the West with the later conquest of the world by the West, in the psychological reactions of nations to foreign penetrating cultures. He did not claim, though, that the fate of the West had to be the same as that of the Greeks and the Romans. Toynbee's accusation put a mirror in front of Europe and raised a lot of questions, the answering of which asked for frankness and an inclination to European philosophy, with its world dimension. But he himself did not answer them.

Nationality & the War. London 1915.
The New Europe. London 1915.
Civilization on Trial. New York 1948.
Die Welt und der Westen. Stuttgart 1953.
Hitler's Europe. London 1954.
Krieg und Kultur. Frankfurt a. M. 1958.
Was heisst geschichtlich denken? Wiesbaden 1960.
Die Zukunft des Westens. München 1964.
Der Gang der Weltgeschichte. Zürich 1970.
The Realignment of Europe. New York 1972.
A Study of History. New York 1995.

VALÉRY PAUL AMBROISE

* 1871 Sète † 1945 Paris

"I am tempted to say - I have to bite back my tongue a little - that Europe represents a kind of system, a unity made up of a certain human diversity and especially positive outer conditions, and definitively formed by a uniquely eventful and lively history. The result of all of these parallel circumstances is a European. ... We, cultural nations, know now that we are mortal. ... An immeasurable horror has shaken Europe to its foundations. It could feel in all the nerve centres that it does not recognize itself any longer, that it has stopped looking like itself, that it has lost its own awareness. ... And now, on a monstrous terrace of Helsingør, extending from Basel to Cologne, neighbouring on the dunes of Nieuport, the moorlands of Somma, the chalk rocks of Champagne, and the granite of Alaska - European Hamlet can see millions of ghosts... . If he touches a skull, it is an enlightened skull. ... And this one is Kant's; Kant engendered Hegel, the latter engendered Marx, and who did Marx engender?"

• French poet, thinker and renowned essayist • studies of law at Montpellier University • 1890 meets A. Gide and S. Mallarmé - influence on his poetry • from 1895 work for the Ministry of War • 1900-1922 employee of a news agency • after 1922 a free-lance writer • 1927 appointed a member of the French Academy • from 1937 Professor of poetics at the Collège de France •

He was - like Spengler - a European of tragic visions. (For example, in his work "The Crisis of the Spirit" he presented a shocking assessment of a collapse of Europe). He spoke about the atmosphere of fear of the coming catastrophe and of the death throes of a European soul, in which educated Europe feverishly experienced its ideas, dogmas, philosophy, ideals, and interpretations of the world and Christianity once again.

According to Valéry, Europe had every qualification to govern the whole world - it had great means and capable people - but those who ruled Europe did not reach the level of its mission and so the European opportunity was wasted on endless and "ridiculous controversies". When he tried to define Europe and a European, he did not want to take the national phenomenon into account, but it was that which proved to be not only inherent but so important for our continent that it nearly destroyed it.

Die Krise des Geistes. In: Corona, Jg. 1, 1919.
Reflections on the World Today. London 1951.
Můj Faust [My Faust]. Praha 1966.
Regards sur le monde actuel. Paris 1973.

VICO GIAN BATTISTA

* 1668 Naples   † 1744 Naples

"And Christian Europe is shining everywhere with humanity that is based on a surplus of all the goods which make human lives happy, give contentment to human bodies and pleasure to the spirit and mind. And all that can exist thanks to the Christian religion, which teaches very sublime kinds of truth, because it has overtaken even the most learned pagan sorts of philosophy and it uses three languages as its own: the oldest language of the world - Hebrew; Greek, which is the subtlest one, and Latin, which is the noblest. Therefore the Christian religion is the best for human aims, since it combines the truth told us by the Revelation with the strength of the reason of the most sophisticated teachings of philosophers and the élite of the knowledge of philologists."*

• Italian philosopher, historian, philologist, poet, and aesthetician • educated by the Jesuits • studies of law at Naples University • governor in the family of the Earl of Vatolle • participation in the Enlightenment cultural movement • 1697-1737 Professor of rhetoric at Naples University • author of philosophical and juristic works • 1725 his work "Principles of a New Science" • 1734 appointed a Royal Historiographer •

He provoked a considerable response, above all by his historical works, in which his debatable opinions on Europe and its role in the world are especially remarkable. According to him, our continent surpasses the other continents in every respect. He appreciated Christianity, which gained recognition for its generally predominating humanist morality, and which therefore seemed to be the best way to the optimum setting of social conditions on the earth. Europe was a rich continent to him, a happy home for all its inhabitants, a union of free states, nations, cities, and villages. Besides the monarchies, that were said to tend towards perfection, there was a large number of admirable republics which did not exist on the other three continents. From these and other points of view, Europe seemed to him to be a near-harmonious continent united by common ideas and an exemplary one for the rest of the world.

Die neue Wissenschaft. München 1924.
Scritti storici. Napoli 1980.
The Course of Nations and the Historical Future of Mankind. Albuquerque 1985.
On Humanistic Education. Ithaca 1993.
New Science. London 1999.
Die neue Wissenschaft über die gemeinschaftliche Natur der Völker.
    New York 2000.
La scienza nuova. Pavia 2000.
Universal Right. Atlanta 2000.
Opere. Milano 2001.

Voltaire (Arouet François - Marie)

* 1694 Paris   † 1778 Paris

"Europe surpasses the other parts of the world in every respect…. For a long time, it has been possible to consider Christian Europe (except Russia) as a large republic divided into various states, one of which is governed in a monarchist way, another in a combined way, some of them in an aristocratic way, others in a democratic one; but all of them influence one another by following the same religious principles, even though they are divided into different sects, and all of them agree with the bases of public law and policy. … Tolerance - that is the only ever-lasting peace which can be made among people. … I can see with pleasure a large republic of cultivated minds being established in Europe."

• French philosopher, poet, playwright, lawyer, and historian • sharp journalist of international repute • from the age of ten he was educated in a Jesuit college of Louis the Great • from 1710 studies of law • 1713 in diplomatic service in the Hague • 1717 sentenced to the Bastille for a pamphlet on Regent Philip of Orléans • on release forbidden to stay in Paris • his first artistic triumphs • 1726-1729 emigration to London - studying J. Locke's and I. Newton's works • 1729-1749 life and work outside Paris • 1749 return to Paris allowed • appointed historiographer at the Royal Court and member of the French Academy • 1750-1753 stay at the Royal Court in Berlin • rich output - poetry, short stories, dramas, satires, pamphlets, historical works, a dictionary of philosophy

• 1753 departure for Switzerland after disputes with the Prussian King
• 1758 return to France • collaboration on the "Encyclopaedia" •

Regarding the unification of Europe, as well as in all other issues, he was extraordinarily critical, often ironic or even sarcastic. And so he responded to the Abbé de Saint-Pierre's plan in the year 1769 by his booklet with the title of "On Eternal Peace - by Doctor Kind-Hearted", in which he described Saint-Pierre's idea as an absurd one, since peace among Dukes is the same as peace "among wolves and dogs". He ridiculed the opinions of Rousseau and others, who saw a solution of human (and European) problems in returning to the "natural" conditions of the old days in the bosom of nature. Voltaire rejected both the idealization of Europe and its being completely condemned, excessive optimism as well as pessimism from the point of view of its prospects, but he saw lots of factors creating the unity of Europe then and in the future, too. He did not link the future of the Continent with the activities of mighty politicians and rulers, but with the advancement of science and culture, both of which were, in his opinion, key factors in European unification, and in accordance with this he was also willing to recognize the mission of Europe for the rest of the world.

Annales de l'empire depuis Charlemagne. Aux Deux-Ponts 1792.
Rozprava o snášenlivosti [A Debate on Tolerance]. Praha 1912.
Nesmrtelné stránky z Voltaira. Jak je vybral a vysvětlil André Maurois [Immortal Pages from Voltaire's works. Chosen and explained by André Maurois]. Praha 1948.
Candide. Praha 1949.
Stati a dokumenty [Articles and Documents]. Praha 1951.
Oeuvres historiques. Paris 1957.
Voltaire myslitel a bojovník [Voltaire - a Thinker and a Fighter]. Praha 1957.
Výbor z díla [Selected Works]. Praha 1978.

WIELAND CHRISTOPH MARTIN

* 1733 Oberholzheim   † 1813 Weimar

"A cosmopolitan is obedient to all the laws of the state in which he lives, whose wisdom, justice and general usefulness are obvious, but he submits to the others out of necessity. He means well by his own nation, but he means well by all the other nations as well and is unable to wish to establish the abundance, fame and greatness of his homeland by favouritism or oppressing other states on purpose. Cosmopolitans therefore do not start working on introducing special unions which would not be compatible with the realization of these ideas. They keep out of any participation in the administration of the state... ."

• German writer of the Enlightenment • 1750 studies of philosophy and law at Erfurt and Tübingen Universities • Professor of philosophy in Erfurt • 1772 governor at the Prince's court, afterwards an official • his initial literary works influenced by the life-style of the Rococo period • in his further works searching for an optimum system for the advancement of man • author of the first novel aimed at teaching humanity to people ("Agathon's Adventures") • 1773 publisher of the "Teutscher Merkur" magazine • 1775 appointed court councillor •

Like Condorcet, for example, he reached over the frontiers of Europe as far as his peaceful and unifying way of thinking was concerned. It was he who introduced terms like "a cosmopolitan" and "cosmopolitanism" (in his works "A Cosmopolitan" and "The Secret of the Order of Cosmopolitans") into our dictionaries not later than the eve of the Great French Revolution. In doing this he did not escape a certain degree of blindness; when considering the merits of European culture and education, he expected the permanent hegemony of Europe over the world. He dreamed of a beneficial revolution not executed "by a wild uprising and civil wars" but in a peaceful, "gentle", convincing way based on reason. He did not disabuse himself of this illusion even after the Jacobin horrors. He made his vision of the unification of European nations clearer still in the year 1798 in his "Talks in Private", where he asked nations to give up their old barbarism, "cannibal" hatred among nations, prejudices, envy, subterfuges, and the "pick-pocketing tricks which used to be called politics". He suggested the permanent existence of a European community and European law court. Later he pinned his hopes on Napoleon, only to experience the worst disappointment of his life, because the Emperor's way was a direct negation of Wieland's ideas.

Der Weltbürger. In: Sämtliche Werke. Leipzig 1818-1827.
Das Geheimnis des Kosmopolitenordens. Ibid.
Gespräche unter vier Augen. Ibid.
History of the Abderites. Bethlehem 1993.
Wielands Briefwechsel. Berlin 1997.

FRANTIŠEK MEZIHORÁK

GALLERY
OF GREAT
EUROPEANS

Language correction Simon and Nora Gill

Published by: NAKLADATELSTVÍ OLOMOUC s. r. o.
Lazecká 70a, Olomouc 772 00
Tel.: +420 585 224 037, 585 204 377
Fax.: +420 585 231 720
E-mail: olomouc@mbox.vol.cz
Internet address: http://www.nakladatelstvi-ol.cz

Printing: Printing office Droždín v. o. s.

1st edition NAKLADATELSTVÍ OLOMOUC, 2003

ISBN 80-7182-149-7